Australia's pioneers, heroes & fools

Dedication

To Worogan, Euranabie, Tommy Winditj,
Jimmy Moorhouse, Charley, Brown, Jackey,
Wylie, Bungaree, Bundell, Yarri, Yagan, Nemarluk,
Pemulwuy and Jandamarra.

They were Bravehearts all, in their own and very different ways.

Australia's pioneers, heroes & fools

THE TRIALS, TRIBULATIONS AND TRICKS OF THE TRADE OF AUSTRALIA'S COLONIAL EXPLORERS

Peter Macinnis

PIER 9

Contents

*Edward John Eyre and Wylie, on the beach in Western Australia —
an iconic picture with a story of its own*

Introduction

Andrew Montgomery was in agony with a spear 8 centimetres into his back. As a surgeon, he could tell that he was losing a lot of blood, and he feared for his life. In August 1821, nobody knew about germs but everybody knew about wounds that went bad, and this one felt very bad. He needed a surgeon's help, but there was only one surgeon on the *Bathurst*—and he was the patient. Montgomery began to wonder if he would die off Australia's northern coast.

It had all started out well enough. Friendly looking Aborigines had come to the beach and beckoned the crew of the small survey brig to come ashore. Gifts had been exchanged: a clasp knife and some fish from the sailors, a possum skin and a club from the locals. Then something went wrong, the Europeans retreated, and Montgomery was speared.

There were no anaesthetics then, other than the rum found on every Royal Navy ship. Usually, the surgeon would dose the victim with rum and operate while the injured man's senses were dulled. This time, there was a catch: the patient–surgeon needed to have his wits about him to tell others what to do, and he could not see his wound. Montgomery had to grit his teeth, hope, and direct his shipmates as they extracted the spear, cleaned the wound and stitched him up.

The crew held out little hope for his survival, so they avenged his expected fate by seizing the possessions of the tribe when they tried the next day to entice the sailors again, and the spear thrower was wounded in the shoulder with a musket ball. Montgomery's long-term fate is unknown, but nine days later, on 16 August, he was on deck when the brig's commander, Phillip Parker King, named the Montgomery Islands, about 300 kilometres north-east of Broome, to commemorate the surgeon's recovery.

Almost a year earlier, King had named Donkin's Hill, some 200 kilometres further to the north-east of those islands, after a manufacturer of tinned meat. This book has its origins in my curiosity about the names that appear on maps, like the Adcock River, named by Frank Hann to commemorate a greengrocer, the man who provided the vegetables for one of his trips. In the Kimberley, they say a creek stays without a name until it is crossed by a road, but on the coast, each point, each bay was laboriously named by the surveyors who sailed around it. There are many, many names, and each one has a story.

A few names date back to the 1600s: in the Gulf of Carpentaria and on the west coast Dutch names may be found, and Broome lies on Roebuck Bay, reminding us that William Dampier once sailed these waters in a ship of that name. Between Broome and Darwin features visible at a distance from the coast often bear French names: Lamarck, Coulomb, Lagrange and other famous scientists are all there, reminding us that the French ships which sailed the area stayed safely and wisely out to sea.

Inshore, the names are more English, commemorating politicians and powerbrokers of many kinds, and those who had offered support to an expedition as well. These were names applied from smaller vessels that could sail close-in. On the land, mountains and hillocks got their names when somebody decided that a feature was a useful reference point to take sightings on to improve the map.

Over time, my interest switched to how people managed to travel through the bush and through the arid centre. This book is therefore not so much the stories of the explorers as a study of the tricks of their trade, the methods they used and the problems they faced, and it is based on the journals that they kept and in most cases published, telling how they survived, mapped and returned.

The mapping of Australia started on the coast in 1606, but until people went ashore and began to fill in the details of the interior, nothing much changed. That means I have told a largely nineteenth-century tale. It's a story of how people used the technology of their time to advance knowledge, science and the acquisition of land, with just a touch of the survival manual about it.

Some of the tricks relate to staying alive, finding food and water, knowing what to take, knowing how to patch up those who were injured or ill. Others relate to methods of finding the way, there or back. Explorers needed to be able to see or find ways through, they needed to draw maps, and they needed to find their way back, which meant knowing where they were. They needed to interact well with the original inhabitants, the Aborigines, who often had good reason not to trust these strange white men.

Of course, not all of the explorers *were* white men. There were many Aborigines who went out to assist the explorers, there were women, a number of teenage boys and even two teenage girls. All of them played their parts in drawing the map and then filling in the charts.

These people are essential to my tale, but there are about 80 of them, and they mostly turn up in several places. Rather than subject my readers to a distracting mess of repetition, I have elected to offer brief pen sketches of them at the end, under *Dramatis Personae* (page 248). There, you will find the main details you need to know, and pointers to key pages where more information will be found— though the best information will be found in their journals, listed in the *Bibliography*. Where I have drawn on these journals, I have retained each author's spellings in all their curious forms.

The stars of this narrative are the land, the environment and the living things that populate it.

✦

I.

The nature of
the explorer

AT EITHER END OF THE NINETEENTH
CENTURY, on opposite sides of the continent, two men
set out to explore bits of Australia. One was under orders
to survey unmapped land for the benefit of European settlers; the
other went out in the hope of finding gold for himself. In between,
many other men and a few women, girls and boys went out to map
parts of Australia but, like bookends, George Evans and David
Carnegie define the limits and nature of the explorer's role on the
mainland of Australia.

Evans went over the Blue Mountains of New South Wales in
1813 to survey the vague route marked out by three earlier explorers,
Blaxland, Wentworth and Lawson, and to map the lands beyond
that point. Evans' account reveals him as a gentle man, keen to make
his mark by serving his fellow humans, and a poor speller who found

genuine pleasure in describing the lands he saw. I suspect I would have enjoyed travelling with Evans, even if important people in London felt his illiteracy made him unsuited to lead exploration parties. They preferred a better class of person who knew Latin, somebody who was born to rule.

Carnegie was just such an upper-class and arrogant young Englishman of the born-to-rule kind. He went out to find gold in the harsh deserts of Western Australia between 1892 and 1897, and any mapping he did was incidental to gold finding. When he finished an epic journey from Coolgardie to the Kimberley, but failed to find payable gold, he wrote his story, starring David Carnegie, and revealed more of himself than was wise. He made classical and literary allusions to show he was one of the educated elite and dropped enough names to remind us he was the younger son of an aristocrat. The mock erudition of this overgrown schoolboy with his contempt for the land and its people cannot match the original thoughts of Evans, the unschooled gentle man with original spelling.

Evans and Carnegie were poles apart in literary skill, charm, tact and social usefulness. They faced different challenges in different terrains and, to be fair, Carnegie had a much harder job, yet many of their tasks, the tools they used and the skills they needed were the same.

Most of the explorers survived, even Carnegie, who died young but in another country. They used the same basic knowledge, shaped by experience, to survive and bring back a record of their travels.

For all that common ground, the experiences of the white-skinned wanderers were varied, as we can see from a few dates in the history of the nineteenth-century bush wandering that most of us unthinkingly call the 'exploration of Australia'. There is nothing special about these dates, except that they show some pretty contrasts and a few trends.

On 27 June 1841, in northern Australia, Captain Stokes of the Royal Navy took whaleboats from HMS *Beagle* into what he assumed to be the waterway named Van Diemen's River by the Dutch. He complained that the prior naming took away the charm of novelty. It seems the novelty would have been retained if the many Aborigines of the area were the only ones who had seen the river. The same day, some 2000 miles (3200 kilometres) south-west, Edward John Eyre and Wylie, his Aboriginal companion and assistant, were ten days away from the settlement at King George's Sound. They had walked around the parched southern coast of Australia from Adelaide, and the plants they saw told them they were getting close. Over three or four years, Eyre walked from one side of the continent to the other, from Sydney almost to Perth, probably the first human to do so. In much the same period, Stokes saw most of Australia's coastline from HMS *Beagle*—but he saw it in rather more comfort than Eyre.

On 24 October 1844, in far northern Queensland, two of Ludwig Leichhardt's companions had strayed and been found by an Aboriginal member of their party. As they set off that morning, the horse carrying the tea fell in a creek, to the explorers' great dismay. Tea was, said Leichhardt, 'unquestionably one of the most important provisions of such an expedition'. On the same day, Charles Sturt was in central Australia, watching with interest how one of his Aboriginal companions killed two dingo pups for food. On the Eyre Peninsula in South Australia, a sculptor called John Theakston was burying his leader, a surveyor called John Darke, who had been 'speared by the blacks'.

Eight months later, on 28 June 1845, Sturt's party in central Australia was trapped by a drought, unable to go forward or back, watching the waterhole at their campsite dwindle. That same night, Aborigines on the Gulf of Carpentaria attacked Ludwig Leichhardt's camp, killing John Gilbert, the natural history collector.

On 5 September 1845, Leichhardt was chasing an emu somewhere near Arnhem Land, and when he jumped from his horse to kill the emu, the horse ran off, scattering possessions far and wide. On the same day, 1000 miles (1600 kilometres) to the south, Sturt found a pretty sheet of water with shy wild fowl that he was unable to kill. In Sydney, surveyor Sir Thomas Mitchell was writing a pompous memorandum to the New South Wales governor, Sir George Gipps, stating that there just had to be a dividing range, west of the Darling River, that there would be a 'great river' beyond, and that he was determined to find it. He never did.

On 14 December 1845, Sturt was in central Australia, being visited by a party of 'very kind' Aborigines to whom he made a present of a sheep, 'which they appeared to relish greatly'. On the same day in 1845, Leichhardt was approaching the end of a trek, accompanied by friendly locals who showed him where to find the settlement at Port Essington, and he was full of regret when they left him. The next morning, Sir Thomas Mitchell left on an expedition that included eight soldiers, because Sir Thomas was sure that any rash explorer who lacked soldiers was courting disaster at the hands of the savages.

On 7 August 1846, three Gregory brothers, four horses and supplies for seven weeks left Toodyay in Western Australia. The brothers lived to become famous for their travels through the bush. On the same day in South Australia, John Horrocks took off with the sculptor John Theakston, a herd of hyperactive goats, an itinerant artist called Gill, a cook named Garlick, a hound for running down emus, and a camel named Harry. Horrocks came home later to die slowly of gangrene, after Harry the camel shot him.

Perhaps we should start there.

‡

HOW HARRY THE CAMEL
SHOT HIS MASTER

Camels helped white explorers travel and survive in inland Australia. In the end, everybody agreed camels were the best animals to use, but it took time to get there because people did not know camels. They distrusted them, they were nervous around these foreign-looking beasts with their habit of appearing witheringly and overwhelmingly superior.

In 1842, Captain Stokes had proposed that camels be obtained from the Gulf of Cutch, where, he said, 'the natives of that part are more easily to be obtained as attendants than Arabs'. Mr Horrocks missed Stokes' advice. If he had known of it, he might have avoided being shot by his camel just a few years later.

Camel people will tell you: first, know your camel, understand your camel's needs and preferences, win your camel's confidence. Be aware, they say, that camels are people as well, but prove it by something more than just dubbing the animal 'Harry'.

In 1846, Harry was the only member of his species on the Australian continent, the last of nine camels brought in from the Canary Islands by an entrepreneur named Henry Phillips. It was probably inevitable that this alien beast, handled badly by people who had no experience with camels, should end up in the possession of John Ainsworth Horrocks, a man equally alien to the Australian landscape, an Englishman who had come to seek his fortune as a squatter in Australia.

We can really only understand the great land grab that happened in Australia by looking at Britain, where possession is literally nine-tenths of the law. If land is unused and you occupy it, and if no claimant objects within a given time, the land is yours. By the time Australia was being settled there might have been a few unoccupied wild moors in Britain, but even these were mostly claimed, and certainly all the best land was held by the descendants of robber barons and others who had stolen most of the land from Anglo-Saxon peasants. It seemed natural to apply similar rules in Australia.

There was a genuine belief in England that Australia was a *terra nullius*, a land almost entirely unpopulated and ready for the plucking, even after the facts proved otherwise. By February 1788, just after the first settlement in Sydney, Watkin Tench, a captain-lieutenant of the Marines and would-be explorer, was ready to question it slightly, while still expressing the belief, based on no evidence, that inland areas would be open for the taking.

> I have already hinted, that the country is more populous than it was generally believed to be in Europe at the time of our sailing. But this remark is not meant to be extended to the interior parts of the continent, which there is every reason to conclude from our researches, as well as from the manner of living practised by the natives, to be uninhabited.

By 1817, any thought that the interior was uninhabited had been shown to be wrong, though numbers were still open to question. John Oxley, the surveyor-general of New South Wales, was told to look into the matter: 'If the people are sufficiently numerous to form tribes, it is important to ascertain their condition, and rules of the society ... ' The general levels of ignorance in Whitehall can be detected in an instruction to Lieutenant Phillip Parker King the following year to determine the inhabitants' 'means of subsistence, whether chiefly, or to what extent by fishing, hunting, feeding sheep or other animals, by agriculture or by commerce'. Fishing and hunting make sense, but feeding sheep as an occupation is about as likely as a corroboree breaking into a rousing mutton-loving chorus of 'All we like sheep' from *The Messiah*!

The instructions came from Lachlan Macquarie, the first governor to make official use of 'Australia', and the text shows a very early use of the formal name we use now for the people who had always been, up until then, Indians or natives. In the instructions, King was told to furnish a 'description of such natives or aborigines of the country as you may happen to see, or fall in with … '

By the late 1830s, large groups of Aborigines had been met in many places, but white settlement now had an impetus that would not be denied, as more and more free settlers arrived hungry for land. More land was also needed for the convicts whose sentences had expired. In Australia, as in America, there was land that manifestly was not under the plough, not fenced, not filled with herds of docile stock—people now knew there were no indigenous sheep.

Clearly, they said, the land was there for any man of daring and resolve to seize, but then you had to persuade the government to let you keep what you had grabbed by squatting on it when the time came for official surveyors to map the area. Horrocks was one of those who moved out into the supposed wilderness, took the best land, and hoped to keep it when civilization and land allocation caught up.

With his brother Eustace, and their faithful butler John Green, Horrocks reached South Australia in March 1839. They were accompanied by other family servants, four merino rams and some sheepdogs. They came well supplied with stores and equipment, and they landed at Holdfast Bay on John's 21st birthday. The Horrocks boys came from a wealthy English cotton-mill-owning family— their grandfather was an influential member of parliament, and had installed the first all-metal power looms and made a fortune out of muslin manufacture.

Their wealthy father paid for 1000 acres (405 hectares) of land in the new colony of South Australia, but the land surveys were in a mess as more and more would-be settlers flooded in. Edward John Eyre had reported excellent land near the Hutt River (where the town of Clare stands today), so Horrocks and the dutiful Green went, looked, and decided to settle there. To make his claim known to others who might arrive in the interim, John Horrocks remained behind, sheltering in a hollow tree, while his loyal butler went and fetched the younger brother, the stores and stock, and the rest of the servants.

The brothers, the attentive Green and the other servants established Hope Farm and a village called Penwortham, after the ancestral home in Lancashire. By 1842, there were 24 people, 3200 sheep, 26 cattle and four horses at Penwortham, but no camels as yet. Writing in 1914, a historian quoted an unnamed source who described Horrocks as 'a young man of splendid physique'. Tall, handsome in a dashing Byronic manner, Horrocks named his favourite greyhound Gulnare after a slave-girl in Byron's *The Corsair*, and he also bestowed the same name on a plain that he passed, thus commemorating his worthy hound's meritorious efforts in that vicinity in catching and killing emus for him to eat in 1841.

He kept an open house, feeding all those who called in for a supper, lodging and breakfast, and he acquired staff from odd sources. One of them, an indigent sculptor called Theakston, he acquired from a debtors' prison, but Horrocks remained slightly aloof, eating at a barrel specially set up for him each night with a clean cloth and a silver fork and spoon. Soon though, Horrocks began ranging further afield, seeking yet greener pastures. In retrospect, taking Theakston along on the expedition may not have been such a good idea, because a couple of years earlier Theakston had been second-in-command to explorer John Darke, when Darke was speared to death on the Eyre Peninsula. Horrocks, however, had no thought of jinxes, and saw only a man with experience in the fine art of exploring.

So it was that John Horrocks set off in late July 1846, with Theakston as his second-in-command, a cook called Garlick, and a 'black boy' (an Aborigine) named Jimmy Moorhouse, goats, horses, dogs, and Harry. They were accompanied by the soon-to-be-famous artist and lithographer S.T. Gill, who came along at no salary to record the expedition. Gill hoped to be able to sell some of his works on his return. Horrocks is featured often enough in Gill's work to make one suspect the painter saw him as a potential customer, but it would never be.

There was also a camel driver named Kilroy, whose task was to manage Harry, for whom Horrocks paid Henry Phillips six cows valued at £90. It was not a good bargain because Harry was not the best natured of animals. While Horrocks modelled himself on Lord Byron in some respects, he was a deeply religious man. Perhaps Harry heard his master citing Isaiah 40:6 and took it literally, treating all flesh as grass, but whatever his reason, Harry often bit people and other animals. He also bit holes in flour bags and engaged in other annoying practices, but mainly he bit people and animals. No sooner had the expedition set out than Harry bit Garlick on the head, badly enough for the cook to need dressing and sticking plaster. In his journal, Horrocks noted that the camel 'had in the morning taken one of the goats in his mouth across the loins, and would have broken his back if Jimmy had not speedily run to its rescue'.

The goats were also a problem: perhaps the occasional camel-mauling made them skittish, but they played up. The explorers had taken goats as a source of meat in preference to sheep, because as Horrocks explained in his journal: 'they give tongue immediately they are caught, so the natives could not take any beast without being heard'. On the night of 31 July, the goats fled the camp, apparently having scented a wild dog, and had to be gathered in from a mile away, but once the adventurers learned to tether the leading goat, the flock stayed with the camp.

The goats had other tricks to play. For starters, all but one of them went lame, and when they decided to move around, they clambered over the tent, ripping it in places, but there must have been more that was left unmentioned because Horrocks recorded killing a goat, 'the one that has given us so much trouble, and which Jimmy was delighted to see slaughtered, having in his hatred to the animal promised Garlick, the tent-keeper, a pint of ale if he would kill it next'. This does not sound like a group that felt comfortable in their dominance over their animals, but worse was to come.

The party pushed on into dry country, leaving their horses behind, but accompanied by the surly camel, which was carrying 356 pounds (161 kilograms) weight. Horrocks, Kilroy and Gill were on foot near a pool that Horrocks had named Lake Gill when misfortune struck. The account that follows was dictated later by Horrocks.

... Bernard Kilroy, who was walking ahead of the party, stopped, saying he saw a beautiful bird, which he recommended me to shoot to add to the collection.

My gun was loaded with slugs in one barrel and ball in the other, I stopped the camel to get at the shot belt, which I could not get without his laying down.

Whilst Mr. Gill was unfastening it I was screwing the ramrod into the wadding over the slugs close alongside of the camel. At this moment the camel gave a lurch to one side, and caught his pack in the cock of my gun, which discharged the barrel I was unloading, the contents of which first took off the middle finger of my right hand between the second and third joints, and entered my left cheek by my lower jaw, knocking out a row of teeth from my lower jaw.

They were, he said, 65 miles (104 kilometres) from the depot where the horses were, with just 5 gallons (23 litres) of water left. Kilroy headed back to Theakston and the horses, leaving Gill to mind the invalid. The artist cared for Horrocks and more: he took dictation from the wounded man, and even painted the scene, with himself lying on the ground outside the invalid's tent, while a slightly sheepish and embarrassed Harry lurks in the background.

Gill also wrote his account of the events:

> The right-hand barrel, with the ramrod in it, went off, taking the middle finger of Mr. H.'s right hand and lodged the charge in his left cheek. He instantly fell back bleeding copiously. We succeeded in staunching the blood with our handkerchiefs, and after cutting off a part of the finger which hung slightly on, managed to dress it with such stuff as we had brought in case of spear wounds, treating the face in the same way; we laid him down, and fixed the tent; after getting him in, Kilroy started back to the Depot the same evening, leaving me in charge of Mr. H. until relief arrived. Soon after Kilroy left, Mr. H. rallied sufficiently to speak, and convinced me that his brain was not affected. We had, of course, a wretched night of it.

Kilroy arrived four days later with Theakston and two horses. Loading Horrocks on a horse and placing a tarpaulin over his legs to keep him there, they set off with Theakston riding the other horse and Gill and Kilroy driving the camel. A week later, they reached Penwortham, where Green the admirable butler dressed his master's wounds, but gangrene had set in and Horrocks died, even after an operation on the gangrenous finger. The infection had spread too far up the arm.

Everybody agreed that Harry the camel had to die for his part in the death of his master. As Horrocks had said before his death, this was not a case of revenge, but so the good name of camels should not be sullied by Harry and his antics. When the first bullet did not kill him, Harry turned and bit the head of Jimmy Moorhouse who was holding him, but a second bullet settled his fate. It is a pity Australians say 'game as Ned Kelly', and not 'game as Harry the camel'—perhaps if Harry had risen to the moment and bitten or shot the man with the gun, we might have a different saying today.

2.

Understanding
the explorers

THE DRAWBACK TO BEING AN EXPLORER WAS that you might end up dead, wounded or terribly sick. The big advantages were the chances for fame and adulation, the explorers' hope of being given a large grant of prime land in any area they found and reported back on, cash rewards, positions of importance, and assorted honours like knighthoods and governorships, or even a peerage as occurred in one instance.

John Forrest became Lord Forrest of Bunbury, probably as much in recognition of his political activities as of his exploration, though he had used his reputation as an explorer to further his political ambitions. There were a number of knighthoods: Major Mitchell became Sir Thomas; while Lieutenant George Grey rapidly became Sir George Grey, governor at various times of South Australia, New Zealand and the Cape Colony; and Charles Sturt was eventually knighted. Eyre became lieutenant-governor in New Zealand under Grey (who treated him abominably), and was then caught up in a scandal in Jamaica that nearly saw him charged with murder. He got out of it, but that was the end of his hopes for a knighthood.

Leichhardt was rewarded by being forgiven a technical desertion from the Prussian army; Oxley was given land. Phillip Parker King became an admiral and a highly respected elder statesman of science in New South Wales, and men of science who visited Sydney made a point of calling at his country estate; but others, like Ernest Giles, who was eventually successful in forcing a way through central Australia down to Perth, were left largely unrewarded, as was scientist and explorer Herschel Babbage.

Some had to settle for getting their name on the map. Horrocks left his name on a pass in South Australia; Darke has a small and lonely roadside monument; Stokes, Giles, Babbage and King are probably known only to enthusiasts. If you asked a well-informed Australian to name some explorers, none of those six would be likely to appear in a national Top Ten. That raises the question: what makes an explorer memorable?

The first thing an explorer had to do in order to gain attention was add to the map of Australia. Most of the names we know today are those who not only produced a journal of their travels, but also had it published. It helped if they did something that involved a lot of suffering. Burke and Wills perished and were admired. Leichhardt disappeared, prompting other parties to go looking for him, but Leichhardt had already been given up for dead once before, then he arrived at Port Essington, so people kept hoping he might emerge from the desert for much longer than they would have otherwise. Eyre and Sturt also managed to be the subject of grave fears before they bobbed up again, much the worse for wear.

Explorers usually were sent out, or arranged funding and went out, with very specific objectives. One was to find land that might be used for farming, though a few went out looking for a way, or a better way, to get somewhere. When Melbourne and Adelaide were established in the 1830s, some tough characters set out from the Yass Plains with stock, hoping to deliver and sell horses and cattle to farmers taking up land near the new settlements. One of them was Edward John Eyre, who learned the rudiments of the exploring trade while taking cattle to Adelaide.

Some pursued scientific specimens. Others went out in the hope of finding minerals like gold or coal. Some sought plants with medical or other commercial uses, or exotic woods that could be used to dye cloth in factories. Perhaps a few of the explorers set out because they were curious to see new places, and no doubt some of them went for the sake of adventure, but in every case they faced a prospect of death that we find hard to understand in our cosseted age of antiseptic surgery, antibiotics, satellite phones, medical evacuations and life support systems. We have to ask: why would they bother? The answer is that they had a different set of values, and from where they stood, the picture looked different.

They might die, but death was more common in their society and something that people accepted more easily than we do. Every member of an exploring party would have seen at least one close relative, a parent or a sibling, die. Most of them completed their journeys before 1870 when the germ theory of disease became an accepted truth to the medical profession, and the last of the explorers had died before antibiotics came into general use. As a result, they approached the risk of death with a fatalism that we find hard to comprehend. Death happened, it could happen anywhere, and every shipload of immigrants travelling to Australia would witness several deaths on board; in a wreck, every member of the ship's company could die, passengers and crew alike. Perhaps the explorers were equally resentful of death when it came, but if they stayed where they were in the city they might still die, and nobody would remember them. So they set off.

INLAND SEAS AND GREAT RIVERS

If they went out with secret hopes of personal fame and riches, they still needed a nobler public reason to go, one that would persuade somebody to carry the costs. There had to be some question that their journey might answer, some prospect of gain for their backers.

The first settlement at Sydney in 1788 was just a toehold, a small village around Sydney Cove that spread where flat land or water allowed. Boats got up to Parramatta, where there was better soil for farming, but this small settlement halfway around the world from where they started out needed to produce food. The colony was desperate for good land, as well as minerals and other things to sell.

The earliest excursions went inland, then up and down the coast, but it took 25 years for the first official journey by Europeans to cross the Blue Mountains that barred any advance to the west. Local Aborigines undoubtedly knew the way over, and it is likely a few convicts did as well, but they weren't talking. Once they crossed the mountains, every explorer found the same thing: there were rivers running west, but nobody could tell where they went. The standard view was that somewhere there had to be a great river flowing into the sea. Later, when nobody could find such a river, people argued that there must be an inland sea fed by the rivers. Logic said the rivers had to go somewhere, and so there must be a giant lake in central Australia, just waiting to be found.

When it comes to writing any *World Book of Great Rivers*, Australia tends rightly to be missed, thanks to the geological fact that the island continent is a thick slab of ancient rock, a single tectonic plate. It is a rather flat slab with almost no mountains to wring water from the passing clouds, but it has plenty of wide plains for the inadequate waters to trickle slowly across, under a baking sun, until they vanish. Much of the water evaporates or soaks into the ground.

Asia has the Himalayas, the Americas have the spine of the Rockies and the Andes, every other continent has high mountains, but Australia just has a line of hillocks dubbed with national pride 'the Great Dividing Range', a chain of ridges dividing the dry part from the arid part. So Australian rivers are generally small, slow, sluggish and given to evaporating before they can get anywhere. Being slow, they are generally hidden behind sandbars and banks of mud where they issue into the sea. The exits can be easily missed despite the most careful scrutiny of the shores.

In south-eastern Australia, the remnant water drifts into the Murray–Darling and feeds gently into the sea behind and around sandhills that hide it from the prying eyes of sailors. The mouth of the Murray is no proud, strong-flowing Amazon mouth, and so the sailors passed it by; the Ord flows mightily in the wet season, but the north coast was no place for boats or ships without engines when cyclones were possible, so it was missed as well.

The nearest thing to an inland sea is Lake Eyre, but the official inland sea theory was for a sea that was fed by the rivers running west from the Great Dividing Range, and all of these, we now know, feed into the Murray or to a Murray tributary. Still, the hope of finding a grand river remained, even when many people had switched to believing in an inland sea, and in 1798, Sir Joseph Banks argued that Mungo Park, a famous African adventurer, be let loose on Australia. Banks wrote to then Undersecretary (not Governor) King:

> Mr. Mungo Park,—lately returned from a journey in Africa, where he penetrated farther into the inland than any European before has done by several hundred miles, and discovered an immense navigable river running westward, which offers the

means of penetrating into the center of that vast continent, exploring the nations that inhabit it, and monopolising their trade to our settlement at Senegambia, with a small force and at an expence which must be deemed inconsiderable when compar'd with the object to be attained,—offers himself as a volunteer to be employ'd in exploring the interior of New Holland, by its rivers or otherwise, as may in the event be found most expedient.

Banks said Park would work cheaply, and that he should be supported by a colonial vessel, which would need to be decked (that is, be more than an open boat), of about 30 tons. He even had in mind a young man to command it, a certain Lieutenant Matthew Flinders, who had by then reached Sydney. For some reason, possibly because the pay was inadequate, Park never sailed on the chosen vessel, the *Porpoise*, and went back to Africa again, which probably saved Flinders from being overshadowed.

✢

FINDING ROUTES

Most exploration parties hoped to find land where crops might be sown or stock bred and fed. Their reports are full of accounts of water, soil, grass, and minerals, but less commonly mention access by land or possible port facilities. This probably represents their lack of success, rather than any lack of effort, but perhaps some of them could not see that far ahead. Maybe they assumed ports and roads would emerge when the need was there.

John Oxley's party had gone west in 1818 from Bathurst, then north, past Dubbo and Gilgandra, at which point they climbed a small hill, grandly dubbed 'Mount Harris', from which they could see the Warrumbungle mountains, more than 160 kilometres to the east. They headed for the Warrumbungles, climbed Mount Exmouth, saw the Great Dividing Range to their east, and set out once more.

Oxley was a former naval lieutenant, so he had looked at the marine maps and decided to follow the Apsley River in the hope that it would lead to a port which appeared at 30°45' south. It seemed likely to him that the Apsley entered the sea there, and while it was shown as a bar harbour—one with a sand bar at its mouth—this was not a worry. He knew that there had been no close examination and that a harbour might appear closed from a distance and yet be accessible. It seemed worth investigating.

They crossed the range and followed the Apsley toward the sea, scrambling down mad slopes, skimming dreadful chasms, crashing through dense scrub, and found themselves facing new problems. The southward route down the coast from Port Macquarie to the settlement at Newcastle included a series of rivers that blocked their way. These were not magnificent streams for penetrating a continent, but they were still enough to make life unpleasant. Still,

Oxley had found new country that farmers and graziers might take up, a way down to the coast that could be improved, and a harbour that could be accessed with some effort. In the days when produce had to go by bullock dray or by sea, it was a welcome contribution.

The 1840s were a time of railway fever, the 1850s saw telegraph fever. Each enthusiasm ended up as a useful technology, just as the Internet emerged unharmed from the 'Dot.com Bubble', but the late 1850s saw men of power and wealth plotting to take a monopoly on the telegraph in Australia and, in particular, the overseas links. Everybody thought India would be connected to Britain in 1859— and it was, briefly, until some of the segments failed. The connection from Singapore to Batavia (Jakarta) was finished, so it was only a matter of time before the telegraph reached Australia, but which colonial capital would receive the news first and control its flow to the other colonies?

The cable might go by sea as far as Brisbane, or it might come ashore near modern Darwin and run to Adelaide, or it might pass into the Gulf of Carpentaria before plunging south, far to the west of Sydney, equally far to the east of Adelaide, all the way to Melbourne, which would then control the traffic and the information. For either overland route to work, a way had to be found, and surveyor John McDouall Stuart spent several years trying to force a route through from Adelaide.

Once we understand that the telegraph was seen as a way to gain wealth and power, we can begin to see why there was such enthusiasm in Melbourne for the Victorian Exploring

Expedition (VEE), which was expected to find a route for the telegraph to come to them, making Melbourne the hub colony. (In fact, even if the line had followed such a route, it would swiftly have gained branch lines to Sydney and Adelaide, losing Melbourne its advantage.) The result of this ill-conceived scheme, however, was a half-cocked parade to the death. Burke and Wills of the VEE reached the salt marshes of the Gulf, but they never made it back alive.

✝

IN THE NAME OF SCIENCE

The habit of collecting specimens began with Joseph Banks, who sailed to the South Pacific with James Cook, collecting plant and animal specimens throughout the trip. He won the favour of King George III, became Sir Joseph Banks, president of the Royal Society, and from this powerful position he supported the seizure and colonization of Australia. He also sponsored many collectors to travel to Australia, either to explore in their own right or to accompany expeditions that were sent out.

Capturing animal specimens was not entirely without risk, as the coastal surveyor Captain Stokes mentioned in his journal. One of the crew spied a snake robbing a bird's nest, with an adult bird trying to scare the snake off.

Mr. Emery immediately climbed up, and with a courage which few other men would have exhibited, seized the reptile by the back of the neck and killed it. We found that it had already swallowed one of the young ones, which had so extended the skin, and made so large a lump, that we were quite puzzled to know how it could have been got down.

The amazing thing is the skill with which new species were apparently detected and identified. Of course, the edited and reworked journals conveniently leave out the mistakes, but when botanist Robert Brown reported the first specimen of a koala in 1803, even if he called it *Didelphis* (possum), he saw it resembled a wombat. It is only in the past 30 years that scientists have agreed to ignore dentition, the arrangement of the teeth, which links the koala to the possum. Like Brown, we now group the koala with the wombat, not with the possum, after getting it wrong for 170 years. Brown wrote to Banks:

A new and remarkable species of *Didelphis* has been lately brought in from the south of Botany Bay. It is called by the natives coloo or coola, and most nearly approaches to the wombat, from which it differs in the number of its teeth and in several other circumstances.

Brown was a trained botanist, and might be expected to notice such fine distinctions, but even the rough and ready bushmen seemed to have an eye for new specimens, though probably many species were sampled more than once as 'new to science'. After all, if closer examination proved otherwise, the 'specimen' could always go in the pot and do the explorers some good.

Collections could be valuable and, as we will see later, Cook's bitter experience showed how a literate crew member might take notes and sell a quick account of a voyage before the official account could be properly drawn up and illustrated. Captains were instructed to collect all notes, sketches and specimens, and collectors were required to sign an undertaking not to jump the gun.

But if the specimens were supposedly protected from theft, they were not always protected from rough handling, as we can see in an 1803 letter from Brown (a botanist who travelled with Matthew Flinders) to Banks:

> The *Porpoise* it seems is so much crowded that she can take but a very small part of the collection of specimens, and even this must be put in the hold. She is, moreover, so wet a ship that I am afraid, small as it is, it may suffer very materially in the passage. The puncheon sent contains specimens of all plants of King George III's Sound and of our five following anchorages on the south coast. The species are not named nor are they very well arrang'd ... I have now to mention a circumstance which has very materially injur'd the object of my mission, which you perhaps, from your own experience, will be less surpris'd to learn than I was to meet with: it is the impossibility I have

experience'd of procuring proper boxes for my collection. On my application to Cap'n Flinders for these during the first cruize, I was told they could not be made then, but that I should have them on our arrival at Port Jackson. In the meantime the plants were put between the beams of the bread-room, where, altho' they remained tolerably dry, yet they suffered very much from mice and insects.

Specimens were still at risk in the mid-nineteenth century. William Carron, a botanist on Edmund Kennedy's ill-fated expedition to travel overland to Cape York, complained that the horse carrying his specimens kept falling in the river, but in the end it mattered little. When the survivors of Kennedy's party were saved in 1848 by a naval rescue party, they needed to run for it, fearing an attack by the local inhabitants.

All my specimens were left behind, which I regretted very much: for, though much injured, they contained specimens of very beautiful trees, shrubs, and Orchideae. I could also only secure an abstract of my journal, except that portion of it from 13th November to 30th December, which I have in full. My original journal, with a botanical work which had been kindly lent me by a friend in Sydney for the expedition, was left behind.

A few years earlier, as his party got close to Port Essington and the end of an epic journey, Leichhardt was forced to abandon specimens, and a little later his party ate the greenhide specimen case. Specimens were important, but getting back alive to tell a tale counted for even more.

✝

THE EXPLORER AS PROSPECTOR

The tradition of the geological explorer is a long one, and from the start the Europeans hunted with a gleam in their eye for any hint of gold or other minerals. Small traces of gold were found and quietly set aside in the early days, so other minerals led the way at first. Still, the colonists were almost as keen to find these lesser minerals, starting with the seams of coal that were exposed on the coast, north and south of Sydney.

Governor King wrote to the Duke of Portland in 1801 about his decision to send a party to what is now the city of Newcastle, to see if the coal there was in commercial quantities:

> The Coal River, 70 miles to the northward of this place, which was seen by a lieut't of the *Reliance* in 1798, and named by him 'Hunter's River,' not having since been examined or any survey taken of it, I was anxious to ascertain how far it might be accessible to vessels, and could be depended on for a supply of coals, and as the service allowed Lieut.-Colonel Paterson's

absence, I accepted his offer of accompanying Lieut. Grant in the *Lady Nelson* on that service.

The colonists were a long way from any merchant who might sell them what they needed. They were naturally more concerned about their own creature comforts, and Grant was delighted to find 'large banks of excellent shells … ', shells which could be 'burned' to make lime that might be used in building. The coal was also good, he said.

It may be imagined that coals were found in great plenty when I mention that the schooner sailed with forty tons, and that we had only one man employed to dig the mine. The spot where these coals are found is clear of trees or bush for the space of many acres, which are covered with a short tender grass very proper for grazing sheep, the ground rising with a gradual ascent intersected with valleys on which wood grows in plenty, sheltered from the winds, forming the most delightful prospect. This place might serve as a station for the woodcutters and colliers.

Before long, Australian coal was being carried to Cape Town on ships sailing back to Britain, but the pace of discovery was too slow for Sir Joseph Banks who wrote to Undersecretary King in May 1798:

We have now possessed the country of New South Wales more than ten years, and so much has the discovery of the interior been neglected that no one article has hitherto been discover'd by the importation of which the mother country can receive any degree of return for the cost of founding and hitherto maintaining the colony.

It is impossible to conceive that such a body of land, as large as all Europe, does not produce great rivers capable of being navigated into the heart of the interior; or, if properly investigated, that such a country, situate in a most fruitful climate, should not produce some native raw material of importance to a manufacturing country as England is.

Here we see another impetus for exploration: London patrons and masters demanded that colonial administrators 'Find More Riches'. Americans had called this attitude 'taxation without representation' and had staged a rebellion, but the home government had failed to learn. They thought they had done the Australian colonies a huge favour by sending some surplus criminals there with a few stores. Now it was up to the descendants to pay dearly for that small favour, and keep paying, generation after generation. The colony was a captive market for British goods but must also provide raw materials, delivered at knockdown prices, taxed and used to feed the growing industrial revolution.

In 1816, when the secretary of state for the colonies, the Earl of Bathurst, instructed John Oxley to be on the lookout for valuables, the instructions singled out 'minerals, any of the precious metals, or stones, if used or valued by the natives'. The following year, the secretary of state instructed Phillip Parker King to 'engage any other person, if there be such in the colony, who possesses a competent knowledge of Mineralogy or Natural History'.

In 1846, Augustus Gregory found coal in Western Australia. He said later that they cut five or six hundredweight of coal with a tomahawk, and so had the satisfaction of seeing the first fire of Western Australian coal. Gregory also found lead, a deposit of galena (lead sulfide), in 1848. It was an exciting discovery, and the governor of the Swan River colony, Charles FitzGerald, could not wait to see the deposit for himself. So off he sailed to Champion Bay to inspect what would become the Geraldine lead mine.

Governor FitzGerald was delighted, but on 11 December, the same day that William Carron traded fish hooks for turtles' entrails on Cape York, and complained that the local people would not leave his camp, the residents of Champion Bay on the west coast wanted these strangers out of their territory. Surrounded and threatened, Governor FitzGerald and two of his soldiers opened fire. FitzGerald killed his target, but the effects of the other shots were uncertain, as the Aborigines were half-concealed in the bush all around the party. Their response, however, was swift.

A shower of spears, stones, kylies, and dowaks followed, and although we moved to a more open spot, the natives were only kept off by firing at any that exposed themselves. At this moment a spear struck the Governor in the leg just above the knee, with such force as to cause it to protrude two feet on the other side, which was so far fortunate, as it enabled me to break off the barb and withdraw the shaft. The Governor, notwithstanding his wound, continued to direct the party, and although the natives made many attempts to approach close enough to reach us with their spears, we were enabled, by keeping on the most open ground, and checking them by an occasional shot, to avoid their attacks in crossing the gullies. They followed us closely for seven miles, after which they were only seen occasionally, following in our track.

The kylies referred to here were boomerangs under their West Australian name, while dowaks are better known across Australia as waddies, or throwing sticks. FitzGerald could have been harmed even more, as it seems one of his ears was nicked by a kylie as it whirled past—an inch or two to the side, and his head would have been badly gashed, or worse.

In most cases, the search for minerals was more peaceful, even if it was less than scientific, but a few principles were beginning to develop. While Stuart's main aim was to find a way across the continent, he kept his eye out for any prospects, and wrote in mid-1859:

> ... we travelled over low rises with quartz, ironstone, and slate; the quartz predominating. Herrgott and Muller, who have both been long in the Victoria gold diggings, say that they have not seen any place that resembles those diggings so much as this does.

At the end of the year, Stuart sank a shaft at Freeling Springs in the northern part of South Australia because he thought he had seen signs of gold in the local quartz. He ended up finding no gold, but took some quartz samples back for closer examination.

One of the major puzzles about the pursuit of minerals is the way a number of prospectors passed over gold in the Kalgoorlie–Coolgardie area, but once you are on camelback, as they were, the answer is clear. Minerals are likely to be found most easily by picking up stones and breaking them, or by chipping bits off rocks. A traveller on horseback can stop a horse and dismount, but a camel needs to hoosh down, to kneel, before the rider can clamber off— and you cannot ask a camel to kneel on a stone-covered plain. One of the first things I learned when poking around the Freeling Springs area with camels was to stay on foot. This also, I might add, reduces the incidence of saddle sores on people, but nineteenth-century prospectors probably knew better than I how to sit in the saddle.

✿

MARKS AND TRACKS

Desert surfaces are fragile, covered in crusts of algae, lichens, clay and minerals. Wheeled vehicles disturb these layers, so tracks made in North Africa in World War II are still visible today. Even carts and drays cut into the surface of a desert, and a land that has only known soft-footed small mammals is permanently scarred when shod horses or hard-hoofed bullocks pass over it.

The first European party to travel through any pristine area left marks that could still be seen plainly years later. Trees chopped or sawn with iron tools look very different from those burned or broken or rotted, and the wheel ruts were clear to even an untrained eye. Others following later would travel on the same path, knowing that route was going to demand less work. With wear, a track sprang up where once no track had been. In time, it would be a road.

Most of the exploring parties took animals. They had horses and camels to ride or to carry loads, cattle as carriers and food, sheep or goats to eat, and when they found good agricultural land, others would soon follow with drays and carts, driving herds of cattle and sheep to the new land, marking the route ever more clearly. And so the roads of Australia were born, winding around trees that stood in the way, edging around projecting rocks because there were too many of them to make it worth shifting them.

Curiously, a number of the explorers thought the soft sandy soils of Australia had been deprived of a good compacting tread from hooves. The land would be fine, they assured their readers, if only it could be trodden down by hoofed animals—and this in spite of the obvious and long-lasting marks they laid down on the parched land they passed over.

The overlanders also left tracks. These men cared little for finding good land, so long as there was enough feed to be had as they passed, so long as it offered a route connecting A with B. The greatest overlanders were probably those taking stock to Adelaide, like Charles Bonney, Joseph Hawdon and Edward John Eyre, who between them opened up new routes linking the settlements of New South Wales with those of Victoria and South Australia. Later, cattle were overlanded to much of northern Australia and, later still, the overlanders became long-distance drovers, retracing their steps and taking cattle to market along what were now well-established stock routes.

We should not be surprised that Australia's rural landscape is criss-crossed by highways bearing the names of those who led exploring parties. As we drive the Hume, Sturt, Mitchell or Oxley highways, we are following, more or less, the path travelled by an explorer at some stage in the past.

Those who actually led exploring parties had a better chance of being remembered, but they were only a small part of the group we call 'the explorers', the people who went out and discovered what was already known, and named what was already named. The one original thing they did was to map Australia, and that gave them the chance to leave their names, and those of their powerful supporters and friends, on the major features dotted across the landscape. They were often less generous in commemorating their travelling companions, and for that reason we often miss the best part of the story.

☧

3 ·
The hidden
explorers

THE HISTORY BOOKS, ESPECIALLY THOSE WRITTEN for school consumption, always leave out the most interesting explorers, the minor ones who sometimes achieved as much as the famous ones but failed to get noticed. It is time to do them justice.

✝

ABORIGINAL EXPLORERS
AND FRIENDS

Captain Stokes noted that when, in 1839, Surveyor-General Roe went out to rescue George Grey's party, who were wandering with no clear purpose along the western coast from Gantheaume Bay (north of Geraldton) down to Perth, there was a 'native who accompanied the party'. By this time, taking Aborigines along was the norm, so they were often left unmentioned or, if they were mentioned, their race was not stated. These men (and very occasional women) were found in most of the parties after about 1830, bringing tracking skills and a deep knowledge of bush conditions.

A few are famous, like Jackey who travelled with Kennedy, and Wylie who kept Eyre alive, but only specialists know of Leichhardt's companions, Brown and Charley; or Warburton's companion who was also Charley; and few will have heard of Tommy Winditj, who was on most of the Forrest expeditions; or Giles' Tommy and Jimmy. Commonly, the Aboriginal members are given European names or referred to simply as 'a native boy' or 'a black' or 'black boy', the term that Alfred Howitt used to describe his assistant when he went searching for Burke and Wills.

A diminutive like Tommy, Charley, Jimmy or Jackey (with no surname) can be a clue, but it is never certain. Young Jimmy Moorhouse is detectable as Aboriginal only because he was described at one point by John Horrocks as 'a native goatherd', but others appear only briefly in the narrative, like 'Kelly and his lubra', who briefly travelled with Horrocks before Kelly left, fearing for his life when Horrocks insisted on travelling into territory where Kelly said his enemies lived.

Some of the Aboriginal explorers have been explicitly identified for us, but only Wylie and Jackey, who saw white companions killed, seem to be famous. Perhaps there is a hint of the 'noble savage' here, the uplifting yarn of the dark-skinned servant who stayed loyally at his master's side. Whatever the reason, some of the more capable assistants are short-changed.

When Tommy Winditj (or Windich) died, he was buried at Esperance with a headstone provided by John and Alexander Forrest. It reads in part: 'He was an aboriginal native of Western Australia of great intelligence and fidelity who accompanied them on exploring expeditions into the interior of Australia two of which were from Perth to Adelaide.'

Bungaree is another under-rated explorer. In June 1801, when James Grant sailed for the Hunter River, he took William Paterson and 'Ensign Barrallier, Mr. J. Harris, six soldiers, two sawyers, a pilot, a miner, and one native'. The 'native' was Bungaree, who became a regular feature on many voyages on the Australian coast. By July 1802, he sailed in the *Lady Nelson* again, as far as Moreton Bay (today's Brisbane), where he found he could not communicate with the local people. At the end of 1817, Bungaree was off around Australia with Lieutenant King and Allan Cunningham, and King described him in these terms:

> ... Boongaree, a Port Jackson native, who had formerly accompanied Captain Flinders in the Investigator, and also on a previous occasion in the *Norfolk* schooner. This man is well known in the colony as the chief of the Broken Bay tribe; he was about forty-five years of age, of a sharp, intelligent, and

unassuming disposition, and promised to be of much service to us in our intercourse with the natives ...

Bungaree also fed the party by spearing fish, at which he was greatly skilled, according to Cunningham, who noted also that, 'Bongaree ... was taken on this voyage at his own particular request.' Cunningham regretted that Bungaree could not understand the language of the Australian north-west, but Bungaree helped in another way, to calm a rather nervous local man on the north-west coast between modern Onslow and Port Hedland. The man ate a piece of ship's biscuit, a bit doubtfully, and happily drank their water, all the while with an eye on Bungaree, who habitually wore European clothing, generally some form of uniform. Eventually, they persuaded Bungaree to strip, to show that he had the ceremonial scars of an initiated man.

They used a naked Bungaree once or twice more as a contact point when they landed, and this may go some way to explain why, after having volunteered and agreed to go with King again in 1821, he had second thoughts, and his place was taken by 'another volunteer, Bundell; who proved not only to be a more active seaman, but was of much greater service to us, than his countryman Boongaree had been', as King reported. Bundell, King said later, was quite willing to remove his clothing, and ride in the bows of a shore-bound boat.

Cunningham called Bungaree 'our native' or 'our friend', but clearly valued the man's assistance in searching for plant specimens, commenting in May 1818:

During the whole of this day's excursion I was accompanied by our worthy native chief, Bongaree, of whose little attentions to me and others when on these excursions I have been perhaps too remiss in making mention, to the enhancement of the character of this enterprising Australian.

Leichhardt had a number of minor discipline problems with Brown, whom he describes as 'an aboriginal of the Newcastle tribe', and rather greater problems with Charley, who hailed from Bathurst. The two Aborigines feuded for a while, and Brown and Charley went out of their ways to win the leader's favour. Leichhardt took advantage of this, playing one off against the other. In the end, Brown and Charley seem to have realized there was nothing to be gained from this and patched up their differences. Brown's morale may have suffered, though:

... our poor dog died, which we all had fondly hoped to bring to the end of our journey. Brown had, either by accident, or influenced by an unconscious feeling of melancholy, fallen into the habit of almost constantly whistling and humming the soldier's death march, which had such a singularly depressing effect on my feelings, that I was frequently constrained to request him to change his tune.

As well as the assistance they had from accompanying Aborigines, the later explorers generally also got help from those they met. In November 1840, Eyre was visited on the South Australian coast by Aborigines who he said were 'not much alarmed'. Eyre noticed that their language was much the same as at Port Lincoln, though also with some words known at King George's Sound, which must have encouraged him to seek a coastal route to the west. After all, if words could travel that implied that people could get through as well.

The visitors were led by a man called Wilguldy, who also told him where water would be found and how to obtain it, and guided him on his way.

> Upon arriving at any of the watering places to which they had conducted us, they always pointed out the water, and gave it up to us entirely, no longer looking upon it as their own, and literally not taking a drink from it themselves when thirsty, without first asking permission from us. Surely this true politeness—this genuine hospitality of the untutored savage, may well put to the blush, for their exclusiveness and illiberality, his more civilized brethren.

Eyre was usually sensitive to cultural differences, but he failed to understand the behaviour of two Aborigines when they shared some roast kangaroo with him and Wylie. The amount of meat was well beyond what they could eat themselves, but by sharing they were storing up a future debt. When Eyre gave one of them a knife that was fine, but these were hunter–gatherers, keen to make the most of good times. Eyre noted that they gorged and then got up in the night to eat again. He put this down to their having no idea of prudence or temperance, calling them improvident. Even the most sympathetic could stumble when faced with trying to comprehend an alien culture.

The supposedly treacherous and savage inhabitants of Cape York helped the worn-out members of the Kennedy party who had been left behind, even as the fitter and more threatening Kennedy was being speared to death. Helpfulness appears to have been the norm, except in cases where the locals had reason to fear the white men, or hate them, on the basis of prior experience. All too often, the intruders made their own troubles.

Part of it came down to courtesy and not being seen as a threat. Leichhardt's party once found themselves among 200 men, women and children and felt no fear, which would seem to have been their companions' reaction as well.

Fear, even obvious fear, could be tempered by gifts. Carron wrote on 16 November 1848, the day the first of his group died, of how the 'natives this day brought us a few small pieces of fish, but it was old, and hardly eatable. I would not allow them to come near the camp, but made signs to them to sit down at a distance, and when they had done so I went to them and gave them a few fish hooks.'

Fear was not only felt by the whites, and John McDouall Stuart offered us some rather interesting insights, when he wrote in 1858:

Our black fellow left us during the night; he seemed to be very much frightened of the other natives. He knows nothing of the country, and if he follows our tracks back, I don't envy him his walk. He was of very little use to us, and I wish I had sent him off before, but I thought he might be useful in conversing with the other natives when we should meet them. He was of no other use than for tracking and assisting in getting the horses in the morning...

Stuart communicated quite well with signs, and succeeded sometimes in getting an indication of where water might be found; given that he learned his craft under Charles Sturt, this is hardly surprising. Looking back later, Sturt could say honestly, 'My path amongst savage tribes has been a bloodless one', and Stuart shared his leader's attitudes.

Ernest Giles seems to have been less sympathetic to Aboriginal culture, but he managed generally to avoid the overtly racist comments of Carnegie, and knew when to seek help. Coming out of the desert while trying to find a way through central Australia to Perth, he and his party persuaded some locals to make them a sand map.

They demonstrated that the Ferdinand, which we had left, and had still on our right or west of us, running south, swept round suddenly to the eastwards and now lay across the country in front of us; that in its further progress it ran into, and formed a lake, then continuing, it at last reached a big salt lake, probably Lake Eyre; they also said we should get water by digging in the sand in the morning, when we struck the Ferdinand channel again.

Giles certainly appreciated the laconic humour of his Aboriginal assistant, Tommy.

On this occasion a tall, gaunt man and his wife, I supposed, were gazing at Tommy's riding camel as she carried the two little dogs in bags, one on each side. Tommy was standing near, trying to make her jump up, but she was too quiet, and preferred lying down. Any how, Tommy would have his joke—so, as the man who was gazing most intently at the pups said, 'What's them things, young man?' he replied, 'Oh, that's hee's pickaninnies'—sex having no more existence in a black boy's vocabulary than in a highlander's. Then the tall man said to the wife, 'Oh, lord, look yer, see how they carries their young.' Only the pup's heads appeared, a string round the neck keeping them in; 'but they looks like dogs too, don't they?' With that he put his huge face down, so as to gaze more intently at them, when the little dog, who had been teased a good deal and had got snappish, gave a growl and snapped at his nose. The secret was out; with a withering glance at Tommy and the camels, he silently walked away—the lady following.

The very first of the seafaring Aborigines, even before Bungaree, seems to have been Yeranabie (or Euranabie), who visited Jervis Bay with his wife Worogan when they sailed with James Grant in the *Lady Nelson* in March 1801. Grant reported with some dissatisfaction that the people of Jervis Bay 'did not thoroughly understand Yeranabie'.

Cook and Banks knew that Aboriginal languages change as you travel, so Grant should not have been surprised at the lack of thorough understanding, though he tells us Yeranabie understood the locals to have said they planned to kill and eat him. Yeranabie was useful at the very least for the colour of his skin. By appearing with the Englishmen, he offered proof that these pale and strangely garbed monsters could be trusted by real humans.

Aboriginal women might have been better as evidence of peaceful attentions, but the mere notion would have been ruled out by most men of the time.

✝

THE FEMALE EXPLORERS

Nonetheless, some women did go exploring. Much of the language in this book is gender-specific. I have written of bushmen, I have depicted explorers as male, and I am not to blame: it reflects the times. However, the early women pioneers were just as tough and resourceful as the explorers. They usually followed close behind and were only rarely in the front line, but there is a difference between 'only rarely' and 'never'.

The women who explored can be found in the records if you know where to look. True, they were few and far between, but that just makes it even more remarkable that these rare cases are so little celebrated. Worogan was neither the grandest nor the first woman explorer.

In the 1800s, ladies of rank might progress some small distance in an adventure. Lady Franklin, wife of the governor of Van Diemen's Land, went on an excursion to the west coast of Tasmania, and explorer, writer and journalist Ernest Favenc described a trip to the Murray that included Colonel Gawler, the governor of South Australia, 'accompanied by Miss Gawler and Captain and Mrs. Sturt'. Favenc apparently could learn no more, noting that he 'presumed that Miss Gawler and Mrs. Sturt accompanied the party but a short distance; the Murray at that date affording anything but a safe camping ground'. A servant girl, Eliza Arbuckle, accompanied them.

The manuscript diary of Julia Gawler, the governor's daughter, reveals that she and Mrs Sturt, while not going on all of the side trips, were there for the whole tour, protected from the mosquitoes by emu-feather fans, and that they also rode out at times and gathered fossils. During their travels, a Mr Bryan rode out with Colonel Gawler to get water. Bryan was unable to continue, and Gawler pushed on. When he returned, Henry Bryan was gone, and never found. Julia Gawler told it like this:

Captain Sturt, Mr. Inman and Bob, set off about 10, to go and look for him, and returned about 6. Said they had found his coat, drawers, handkerchief, stiffener, telescope, saddle, bridle, blanket, socks, and a bit of paper on which was written: 'Sunday evening, 9 p.m. Gone in S. S. E. direction, could not go on sooner through exhaustion. H. Bryan.'

It was, as they were fond of saying in those times, no place for a woman, but some of the women did not listen. Favenc would have known more than a little of women explorers because he travelled with one. Emily Creaghe was 22 and pregnant for the second time (she had lost the first child) when she spent six months working around the Gulf of Carpentaria as a member of his party.

She travelled to Bowen by steamer in late 1882, then on to Normanton, and was pregnant when they set out for Darwin. Along the way, she suffered 'Gulf Sandy Blight', or ophthalmia, which left her with only half an eye, but she was still able to witness some fairly severe treatment of Aboriginal people before she reached Port Darwin and gave birth to a son in January 1884. By then, though, women had been exploring in Australia for almost a century.

The first of the women explorers was 'Louis Girargin', in reality the 38-year-old Marie Louise Victoire Girargin, the ship's steward on the *Recherche*. She visited Tasmania in 1792–93 and her gender must have been a fairly open secret; it is likely that both Bruny d'Entrecasteaux and Huon de Kermadec were aware of her status, as she had a separate cabin. All the same, she tried to keep it a secret and even fought a sword duel to demonstrate her masculinity, suffering a gashed arm in the process of becoming the first woman to fight a duel on Australian soil. She apparently later became the lover of a sub-lieutenant, but they both died of dysentery in 1794.

Then there was Rose Freycinet, who was airbrushed out of history after she had voyaged with her husband for three years, from 1817 to 1820, and had her name given to a Samoan island. She stowed away with the connivance of the captain (her husband), and was the only woman among 125 men throughout the voyage. She was disguised as a man only for the first few days.

The episode came out after the *Uranie* was wrecked in the Falkland Islands, but Louis de Freycinet seems to have suffered no punishment, though the matter was somewhat hushed up. There is a watercolour of Shark Bay, painted by Alphonse Pellion in 1818, showing Rose sitting on the shore, but when this was reproduced in the official report Rose was no longer in the picture. In those days, every painting needed to be engraved, allowing such blemishes as unofficial women to be quietly deleted at that stage.

THE JUVENILE EXPLORERS

The commander was less involved in the stowing away of an unnamed girl who was found upon Phillip Parker King's ship at the end of May 1821. The ship was three days out of Sydney when the hold was opened.

> ... a young girl, not more than fourteen years of age, was found concealed among the casks, where she had secreted herself in order to accompany the boatswain to sea: upon being brought on deck, she was in a most pitiable plight, for her dress and appearance were so filthy, from four days' close confinement in a dark hold, and from having been dreadfully seasick the whole time, that her acquaintances, of which she had many on board, could scarcely recognize her. Upon being interrogated, she declared she had, unknown to all on board, concealed herself in the hold the day before the vessel sailed; and that her swain knew nothing of the step she had taken. As it was now inconvenient to return to put her on shore, and as the man consented to share his ration with her, she was allowed to remain; but in a very short time heartily repented of her imprudence, and would gladly have been re-landed, had it been possible.

The voyage lasted some eleven months, but there seems to be no other record of this adventurous young lady, or what later became of her. Of the teenagers who travelled with Sturt to the Murray, the fate of Henry Bryan, who died at eighteen, is a mystery to this day, though Julia Gawler, aged fifteen at the time of the excursion, later married a George Hall. Eliza Arbuckle, a nineteen-year-old, also survived and later married before moving to America.

Jimmy Moorhouse seems to be an exception to the naming rule. He was both young and Aboriginal, yet he was not only given a surname, but also mentioned in the records. Perhaps the difference is that John Horrocks' account was never edited for publication, just put into print in its raw form, but while we know his name and some of his actions, all we know is that Jimmy was 'a boy'.

John Murphy was a teenager who travelled to Port Essington with Leichhardt, and made himself useful as a collector. He paid for his devotion to botany when he tried to preserve a specimen of a new *Grevillea*. Known as the spider flower, the genus is popular in Australian gardens, but infamous among susceptible Australians for the rashes it causes. Murphy learned about it the hard way, because he lacked pockets in his 'trowsers'. He had already put a number of prickly seeds of *Sterculia* inside his shirt for safekeeping. Then he saw 'the drooping *Grevillea*' in fruit, and tucked some branches of that in his shirt as well.

> Upon arriving at the camp, he felt great pain; and, on examining the place, he saw, to his greatest horror, that the whole of the skin of the epigastric region was coloured black, and raised into a great number of painful blisters. Upon his showing it to me, I thought that it was caused by the *Sterculia* prickles having irritated the skin, and rendered it more sensitive to the sharp properties of the exudation of the seed-vessels of *Grevillea*. Brown, however, merely touched the skin of his arm with the matter, when blisters immediately rose;

showing clearly its properties. The discoloration of the skin was like the effects of nitrate of silver.

George Grey had a boy with him during his wild and woolly exploits. On his first trip, Grey had a ship drop him on the northern coast near the Kimberley, far from the nearest settlement at Perth, where he bumbled around (and was speared) before making contact with the ship once more. In his second trip, Grey planned to search along the west coast to find the large rivers that simply *had* to be rolling into the ocean, carrying the waters that would otherwise have pooled in an inland sea.

The expedition started out in February 1839 in an American whaler, taking three whaleboats with them. The party of twelve landed just north of Shark Bay on Bernier Island, and the whaling ship left, taking all of the tobacco with them and generating an early taste of despair. There was no water on the island, and their first attempt to leave it saw a boat smashed and nearly half a ton of stores lost. They made it to Dorre Island, where they were hit by a storm, but eventually they got to the mainland.

A string of blunders followed and, at the end, the party was strung out along the coast, indicating a total lack of leadership on the part of Grey. According to Favenc, they 'had been then three days without any water but sea water, and a revolting substitute, which they still had in their canteens' (presumably their own urine).

Grey took off with insufficient water, because of a misplaced faith in the rivers that *must* be there. He was a cocky young army officer, keen to have adventures and make a name for himself—and in the end, a youth died from that misplaced faith made worse by cockiness.

John Septimus Roe, once Lieutenant King's midshipman, was now a mature and hardened bushman, the surveyor-general in the colony of Western Australia. He went out to rescue the remnants of Grey's sad party. According to Stokes, who had the details from Roe, Grey had left one of their number, Frederick Smith, behind before Roe met up with them, 'and so bewildered were they in their despair, that they could give no definite account of what had become of him'.

They had been struggling down the coast, heading for Perth, but Roe's rescue party found Grey's people on a beach, blocked by a rocky headland that they lacked the strength to climb over. Ernest Favenc pointed to this later as evidence of the need for explorers to be qualified. He seems to have been far too gentle, for Grey's deficiencies went well beyond an 'occasional want', but perhaps he realized that Grey was both still alive, and influential, when he wrote:

> Grey's mishaps, and the straits to which he reduced his party by his occasional want of forethought and precaution, show plainly that enthusiasm, courage, and a generous spirit of self-sacrifice are not the only requisites in an explorer, more important even, being the long training and teaching of experience.

I suspected at one stage that the unlucky Smith might have been a convict, but Grey adorns his name with 'esquire' at one point and refers to him as a 'young gentleman' at another. Grey mentioned later that Frederick Smith was the grandson of a member of parliament, and had gone to Australia to adventure with Grey. If he *had* been a convict explorer, he would by no means have been the only one.

✜

THE CONVICT EXPLORERS

Some of the earliest explorers were criminals of one sort or another. Indeed, the first two Europeans known to have lived for any length of time in Australia were two convicted criminals stranded on the shore by Francisco Pelsaert in 1629, but we have no idea what, if anything, they learned before they perished.

Within a few days of the First Fleet landing, some of the British convicts were out wandering the bush, in part because French ships were anchored at Botany Bay and a few of the felons hoped for a quick ride home again in one of them. There is a modern Australian belief that the French arrived out of the blue, and that if the First Fleet had not arrived when it did, the French would have claimed Australia for themselves, and Australians would consume more croissants for breakfast.

Perhaps La Pérouse might have made a territorial claim, even though James Cook had already done so in 1770, but the French were not in Botany Bay to settle or to claim any sort of dominion.

They came into Botany Bay to recover from storm and other damage that had been sustained during an exploring mission. And they did not come entirely unexpected, as we can see in this entry from the journal of Philip Gidley King on 24 January 1788:

> The 24th, in the morning, two strange ships were discover'd to ye southward of Cape Solander, and we soon after discover'd that they were French, one of which wore a *chef d'escadre*'s pennant, from which we conclude them to be *La Boussole* and *L'Astrolabe,* under ye orders of Monsieur de La Perouse, on discoveries, but the wind blowing strong from N. N. E. prevented their getting in or our going out.

That deduction, of course, scuttles the 'arrival out of the blue' line, because just by detecting the commodore's flag, the naval officers were able to deduce not only the ships' names but also the name of the commander. In short, even if the French did not expect to meet the British at Botany Bay, the British certainly expected those particular Frenchmen to be in the area.

It made for a slightly difficult situation, though, because the First Fleet was about to set off for Port Jackson, Sydney Harbour, just as La Pérouse sailed in. All in all, that was probably good, because some of the convicts would most certainly try to escape in the French ships, so if the French were in Botany Bay, and the British were in Sydney Cove, that would put an end to that, surely?

In reality, the deserted shore was anything but deserted, and the people of what we now call La Perouse, on the northern shore of Botany Bay, were also the people of Sydney Harbour, and over the millennia, their feet had worn clear tracks through the bush from one harbour to the other. Soon the convicts had, in Watkin Tench's words, 'found the road to Botany Bay', where they implored the French to give them passage. It did not wash, but now the Frenchmen realized there was a path joining the two harbours, and Arthur Bowes Smyth, who was a First Fleet surgeon, wrote on 19 February 1788:

> This day 3 of the Frenchmen from the ships w'h lie in Botany Bay came here overland w'h fowling-pieces, under the pretence of shooting, but I rather think they came to take a view of the matters going on here. They have already erected a fort w'h 2 or 3 guns on shore at B. Bay. The Governor has forbid any one going over to Botany Bay. Two horses were sent over to conduct the French commodore and suit here.

Another popular myth is that many of the convicts believed that they were close to China, that they could easily make their escape by slipping over a few hills. Perhaps they believed it for a while, but before long there was more interest in a mythical colony of white people, vaguely located three or four hundred miles south-west of Sydney. There even written travel instructions circulating, complete with a compass rose to make them appear genuine.

Governor John Hunter worried that many gullible convicts would die in agony or end up returning to an almost equally agonising punishment. He declared that four men, picked by the convicts, were to be taken on the route shown on the map by three experienced bushmen, so they might see that the hope was forlorn. The convicts were determined not be fooled by the governor. They conceived a cunning plan to hijack the expedition, with a larger body absconding, murdering the guides and then proceeding to the safety of the fabled white colony. Luckily for them, this scheme was uncovered and four soldiers were added to the party, scotching the plot.

One of the guides was a former convict named John (or James, according to some accounts) Wilson, who had spent some time with the Aborigines. He had been given an Aboriginal name and it was said his body was 'marked and scarred after their fashion'. Wilson told tales of wonders he had seen in the bush, and was widely regarded by the whites of Sydney as a liar, but he knew his way around the bush, so he went with the party when they set out on 14 January 1798.

Ten days later, the soldiers returned with three of the convicts. The soldiers had been instructed to return when they reached the foot of the mountains, but the three convicts said they had seen and suffered enough, and begged to be allowed to return with them. The rest of the party arrived at Prospect Hill, on the outskirts of the settlement, on 9 February, praising Wilson for keeping them alive.

The first convict expedition achieved little. They kept no clear record of where they had gone, though they said they had seen creeks and a large river. They claimed to have met few natives, but those they saw were dressed in skins from head to foot (unlikely in summer), and they reported seeing a fat mountain wallaroo. They returned with a specimen of a lyrebird and reported dining on 'a kind of mole', apparently a wombat, but that was the limit of their achievements.

Wilson died soon after, speared by Aborigines for an infraction of their customs. (As an initiated man, he was expected to know and obey these customs, but it seems he did not.) In him, Australia lost either a good bush wanderer or an excellent storyteller, or maybe both.

In the first official crossing of the Blue Mountains, Blaxland mentioned taking 'four servants, with five dogs, and four horses laden with provisions, ammunition, and other necessaries'. A servant, whether a convict or a free man, was merely hired labour, and as these servants had expressed misgivings and asked to go back, he had perhaps even less reason to give them any credit. All the same, three of his 'servants' were convicts.

There were probably more convicts and ticket-of-leave men in the various expeditions, but rather than being listed by their state of servitude, party members were usually listed more by their role during the expedition, appearing in the records as 'farrier', 'gardener', 'boat-builder', 'harness mender', 'with the sheep', 'for chaining with surveyors', 'mineralogist', 'butcher', 'botanist', 'loader of packhorses', 'bullock driver', 'shoemaker' and 'surgeon'; while the military surveyor-general Major Mitchell included 'mounted videttes', a 'barometer carrier', 'chainman', 'carter and pioneer', 'tent-keeper' and 'store-keeper', among others.

Some of the early explorers who were born and raised in Europe had problems when it came to travelling in Australia. They followed river valleys, because they were used to glaciated landforms where the valleys were broad and easy to walk along. In the old Australian geology, where chasms had been carved by millennia of rare floods, that was not a good move. The valleys were steep-sided and hard to get out of, and the narrow defile at the bottom was usually blocked by rock fragments that had tumbled down at some point after the valley was last carved. Worst of all, there was usually no crystal stream gurgling along, as there would be in any decent European valley.

In the same way, based on what was known of other continents, Major Mitchell, like Banks, Grey and others, was willing to believe in the myth of a great river, stretching across the continent, even though careful mapping of the coast had failed to reveal the mouth of any such river. He had been told by a liar that the river existed, and that was enough for him.

It began with a wild tale from a runaway convict called George Clarke, otherwise known as 'the barber'. Clarke had been living with Aborigines, and had the scars of an initiated man, but he had been stealing cattle. Recaptured and questioned, he said he had heard of a river called the Kindur, running to the north-west, and he said he had decided to follow it, hoping to reach another country. Ernest Favenc argued plausibly that Clarke's yarn was fabricated to save him from a flogging when he returned but, naturally enough, Clarke the barber claimed that it was all true.

Clarke said he had started at the Liverpool Plains, and followed a river which the natives called the Namoi. Along the way, the River Peel, the river that Tamworth lies on and that Oxley named, joined in. Clarke had crossed the Namoi and reached what he took to be the Kindur, which he then followed for 400 miles (640 kilometres) before the Namoi joined it. The river was navigable and flowed on, he said. He was not sure how far it went, but he said it never flowed to the south of west. In other words, here was a perfect path to strike off up into northern Australia, a marvellous river on which to progress toward great riches.

The government fell for it, as governments will, because they wanted to believe. The acting governor of New South Wales, Sir Patrick Lindesay, sent Mitchell out to investigate in November 1831. He went across the Peel, over the Hardwicke Range, and reached the Namoi River about three weeks later. Expecting a navigable waterway, the party had come equipped with canvas boats, but these snagged in the river, so the party reverted to horseback. They reached the Gwydir, turned west along it for some 80 miles (128 kilometres), then struck north to a grand river known locally as Karaula. Mitchell followed this down till the Gwydir joined it and, given that it was heading south, deduced that this was Sturt's Darling River.

All the same, if the Kindur River was a non-starter, the rivers had to flow somewhere, so the prospect of an inland sea remained good. Just as the Greek and Roman originators of the European culture once saw their world as surrounding the Mediterranean Sea, so the new Australians dreamed of a continent surrounding an inland sea, with snow-capped alps somewhere about the Gibson Desert—but not everyone was convinced. Eyre certainly was doubtful.

Keep in mind that Eyre had tried to reach central Australia along the line of the Flinders Ranges, and had fallen back. He had set out around the Great Australian Bight because he hoped to find, at some point, more gentle and welcoming country to his north, so he could turn right and reach a land of milk and honey. It was not to be, and wilting under the ferociously hot northerlies which he likened to the blast of a furnace, Eyre wrote:

> There was no misunderstanding the nature of the country from which such a wind came; often as I had been annoyed by the heat, I had never experienced any thing like it before. Had anything been wanting to confirm my previous opinion of the arid and desert character of the great mass of the interior of Australia, this wind would have been quite sufficient for that purpose. From those who differ from me in opinion [and some there are who do so whose intelligence and judgment entitle their opinion to great respect], I would ask, could such a wind be wafted over an inland sea? Or could it have passed over the supposed high, and perhaps snowcapped mountains of the interior?

In time, Australian-born explorers would cease to be a minority. More importantly, those Europeans who believed they were born to lead would be replaced by men like Hume, Eyre, the Forrest brothers and the Gregory brothers, supple-minded explorers who were either born in Australia or born elsewhere but who had learned to relate to the country as John Wilson and George Evans had done. They knew the bush, and they read the bush.

Back to the criminal pathfinders though: one famous explorer died believing he was at least technically a felon. As Ernest Favenc told the tale:

> Leichhardt was born in Beskow, near Berlin, and studied in Berlin. Through a neglect, he was excluded from the one-year military service, and thereby induced to escape from the three-yearly service. The consequence was, that he was pursued as a deserter and sentenced *in contumaciam*. Afterwards, Alexander Von Humboldt succeeded, by representing his services to science on his first expedition in Australia, in obtaining a pardon from the King. By a Cabinet order Leichhardt received permission to return to Prussia unpunished. This order, whether of any value to Leichhardt or not, came too late. When it arrived in Australia he had already started on his last expedition.

One of Leichhardt's companions on his earlier trip to Port Essington was a genuine prisoner of the Crown called William Phillips, who later received a pardon and £30 for his services. During the journey, Leichhardt named a peak Phillips' Mountain, 'after one of my companions', but Phillips remained a little aloof, perhaps being conscious of his position.

> ... he erects his tent generally at a distance from the rest, under a shady tree, or in a green bower of shrubs, where he makes himself as comfortable as the place will allow, by spreading branches and grass under his couch, and covering his tent with them, to keep it shady and cool, and even planting lilies in blossom [*Crinum*] before his tent, to enjoy their sight during the short time of our stay.

THE BUSHRANGERS

The first 'bush rangers' in Australia were literally men who ranged the bush, like Hamilton Hume, seeking good land for settlement. It appears that this was the standard American term for this sort of person—some of those in the First Fleet had spent time in America, and a number of American terms were transported to Australia, along with the convicts. This explains the American opossum having an Australian counterpart in the possum, the Australian goanna (derived from the American iguana), and the frequent references to the established Australian residents as 'Indians'. Australia was just as much a new world as America was to the Europeans who found themselves on its shores, and they grasped for analogues and parallels.

In time, 'bush ranger' came to be a single word with a new meaning. The later 'bushrangers' were villains who stole to stay alive, and who used their bush skills to escape the troopers, the mounted police who were sent after them. We can see the earlier use in an account by Governor King, written in 1805, in which he described how an expedition of bushmen had failed to cross the Blue Mountains, to the obvious disgust of the governor, who mentioned their supposed travels and concluded:

> From thence it appears they were tired and returned to Hawkesbury. The whole of their story is so contradictory that I should not have inserted these particulars but to prove what little confidence can be put in this class of what is locally termed bushrangers.

Even after 'bushranger' took on its negative sense of robber, bandit or runaway convict, there were men who ranged the bush, probing for new land in new districts. These, the true bush rangers, were generally people who had been brought up in the bush and who understood it, and they were generally among the first to reach new lands, often ahead of the official explorers. But these days, the Beardies of Armidale, William Chandler and John Duval are lucky to rate a mention in local histories, and who has heard of Nat Buchanan?

Whoever they were, known or unknown, the explorers needed to learn from somebody. The bush rangers learned a little by venturing short distances into the bush, they learned from people like Wilson and Clarke, who learned from the Aborigines. After that, the explorers learned from each other—and because their lives might hang on learning well, the pupils paid close attention ... or died.

4 ·

First, train
your explorer

ARLY NAVAL EXPLORERS KNEW HOW TO MAP COASTLINES, and their methods were learned and passed down. William Bligh sailed with James Cook and Bligh later commanded Matthew Flinders, who had John Franklin in his crew and also inspired Phillip Parker King to go exploring. John Septimus Roe, later a surveyor and land explorer in Western Australia, sailed as a midshipman with King. Stokes, who had met King in Tierra del Fuego while he was on the *Beagle* with Charles Darwin, was welcomed in Hobart by the governor, now Sir John Franklin, who later died seeking the North-West Passage in a company that included brothers of both William Wills, of the ill-fated Burke and Wills expedition, and Alfred Gibson, who died in Gibson's Desert while out with Ernest Giles.

The same links can be found among the land explorers. John McDouall Stuart first went out with Charles Sturt, who had made his first trip with Hamilton Hume, who had gone out ranging the bush as a boy with young friends and his older brother, John. Young Hume gained much of his mapping experience from surveyor James Meehan, with whom he travelled in 1817. Sturt was also a good friend to both Edward John Eyre and Augustus Gregory, and there are many other cases of explorers meeting and talking to each other. Then again, most of the early explorers published journals of their travels, partly for posterity but also so that other explorers could gain from their experience—if the journals were completely truthful.

The men of science and medicine also played a part. Surgeon John Harris went to the Hunter River with Barrallier, Grant and Paterson in 1801. In 1817, George Evans and Harris (then in his sixties) both travelled down river by boat from Bathurst with John Oxley, and then across the plains and mountains to the coast. Soon after, Allan Cunningham sailed with Phillip Parker King. At various times, George Caley, John Gilbert and Ferdinand von Mueller were all associated with other explorers. However you look at it, there were plenty of opportunities for the scientists to pass on what they had learned and train those with less experience.

When Watkin Tench went to see what lay west of Sydney, there was no tradition of land exploration to draw on. Tench later emphasized the hardships for a British readership, though his problems were no doubt real enough at the time.

But before we set out, let me describe our equipment, and try to convey to those who have rolled along on turnpike roads only, an account of those preparations which are required in traversing the wilderness. Every man [the governor excepted] carried his own knapsack, which contained provisions for ten days. If to this be added a gun, a blanket, and a canteen, the weight will fall nothing short of forty pounds. Slung to the knapsack are the cooking kettle and the hatchet, with which the wood to kindle the nightly fire and build the nightly hut is to be cut down ... Thus encumbered, the march begins at sunrise, and with occasional halts continues until about an hour and a half before sunset. It is necessary to stop thus early to prepare for passing the night, for toil here ends not with the march. Instead of the cheering blaze, the welcoming landlord, and the long bill of fare, the traveller has now to collect his fuel, to erect his wigwam, to fetch water, and to broil his morsel of salt pork. Let him then lie down, and if it be summer, try whether the effect of fatigue is sufficiently powerful to overcome the bites and stings of the myriads of sandflies and mosquitoes which buzz around him.

Tench later explained how he and his fellow officers kept track of their path in the wilderness in April 1791. The 'traverse table' that he mentions in the following discussion was probably a traverse board, which was commonly used on board ships and which had pegs and holes. Each half-hour of a four-hour watch, a peg would be placed to summarize the direction travelled during that time, while a second peg would record the speed in knots.

> Our method, on these expeditions, was to steer by compass, noting the different courses as we proceeded; and counting the number of paces, of which two thousand two hundred, on good ground, were allowed to be a mile. At night when we halted, all these courses were separately cast up, and worked by a traverse table, in the manner a ship's reckoning is kept, so that by observing this precaution, we always knew exactly where we were, and how far from home; an unspeakable advantage in a new country, where one hill, and one tree, is so like another that fatal wanderings would ensue without it. This arduous task was always allotted to Mr. Dawes who, from habit and superior skill, performed it almost without a stop ...

In other words, the early travellers kept track of the direction with a compass and the distance by counting paces, then combined the distances and directions to produce a rough map of where they had gone. In later years, it was common to estimate distances and record those and the bearings every ten or fifteen minutes, so the whole path could be plotted at the end of the day, assuming an established average speed. The ideal, though, was to draw a map that had major landmarks accurately plotted.

‡

THE ART OF THE MAP

The Aboriginal people of Australia may not have had paper, but they most certainly understood mapping and landmarks. Some of them even made sand maps to show their white visitors what lay ahead of them, but the notion of a unified scale map of a whole continent was as far from Aboriginal minds as it was from Aboriginal needs.

The people we call explorers entered areas of which they had no knowledge, risking unknown but wildly imagined dangers. Paradoxically, the early explorers called the unknown land 'desert' before they reached it, implying that it was deserted of all human life, but at the same time they feared the 'wild savage' who, they believed, might suddenly appear, hurling spears at them when they considered themselves to be passing harmlessly by.

Many surveyors and mapmakers understood why they could be seen as a threat, they knew that the land was far from deserted and often sought out the local inhabitants. Most importantly, many of them made a real effort to make themselves more welcome—though not all of their attempts were equally successful. That, too, was an art that had to be learned.

Starting from almost complete ignorance, the wanderers needed to find a negotiable way and map it, but there was more to the challenge than jotting notes of conditions, events and measures in a field notebook and making charts. As well as needing skills in surveying, measuring and mapping, the explorers had to find their way, catch or gather food, and locate water and shelter. They needed skills and knowledge which in this day and age are probably possessed only by a small minority of hardened bushwalkers.

Travellers in new country needed at least a passing knowledge of plant and animal taxonomy: it was useful to be able to recognize bird species since they often showed where water was. They also needed to know about meteorology, geology and mineralogy, surveying, astronomy, navigation, tracking, blacksmithing, animal-wrangling, surgery and medicine for both animals and humans, needlecraft in canvas and leather, diplomacy and anthropology. They had to be good shots, able to find water in an arid landscape, and to be willing to eat and drink whatever food and water they could find. The main thing was to get out there, create reliable maps and marks for others to follow, and get back home with their hides, their maps and their other records intact.

FILLING IN THE OUTLINE MAP

The first maps of Australia showed the coastline, as drawn from the sea. Ships and boats worked their way around, producing an outline map, but it was an outline with extra details. In 1848, while he was working the area north of Geraldton in Western Australia where Grey's party came to grief, Augustus Gregory had a clear view of mounts Peron and Lesueur, which had been named from the sea by Nicolas Baudin almost half a century earlier. Assuming Baudin had placed them correctly on the map, Gregory could then use bearings on the two peaks to locate himself accurately, by drawing back-bearings on the map, knowing that his location was at the intersection of those two lines. This in turn would locate him in relation to the coastal features shown on the chart, even if they were out of sight.

That raises the question of how people out at sea could plot inland mountains, especially when sailing ships needed to keep a healthy distance from the coast to be safe from winds, reefs, tides and currents. The answer is that they did a running survey, taking bearings on key points at regular intervals, while estimating the ship's speed. Later, these measures could be combined with the occasional latitude and longitude determination to join up the fixed points and produce a chart that summed up all the main features, a chart that was consistent with all of the observations.

If the shipboard explorers also took bearings on the two mountain peaks as they appeared to line up with several remarkable coastal features, then the intersections of those lines on the chart located the mountains themselves, even if they were far from the sea. In this context, 'remarkable' meant a feature was sufficiently different to be recognized from many angles. Kangaroo Island's granite tourist attraction, Remarkable Rocks, got its name that way.

Once you have some points identified, named and located on the map, you are ready to fill in the map, using a handy piece of mathematics familiar to the ancient Greeks: if you know any two of the angles in a triangle, you can work out the third, and given the angles, if you know how long one side is, the rest can be calculated.

This is why mounts Peron and Lesueur were so useful: they were marked on a scale map, so Gregory could use the map to measure their distance apart, then stand on another mountain and take bearings on them. After that he just needed a protractor and a straight edge to plot the position of his mountain.

Over time, small errors would creep in, but you could correct at least the north–south errors by taking sightings on the sun and the stars to get the latitude, and you could even use a complicated method called 'lunars' to estimate the longitude. We will come to the lunars later.

The greatest joy for any surveyor was always to 'connect the survey', which meant joining up the measurements, either back to the starting point or to known and established fixed points. Even before reporting some June 1817 results, Oxley wrote in his journal, 'Bearings were taken to several remarkable hills for the purpose of connecting the survey.' Then in July, he gloated:

> I came back to the tent at half-past four o'clock and it was extremely satisfactory to us to find, on laying the different bearings down on the chart, that the connection of the survey with Mount Aiton corresponded to less than a mile of

longitude, although it had extended on a most varied course from that point between three and four hundred miles.

What this means is that either the measurements were remarkably accurate throughout, and all consistent, or perhaps there had been same degree of compensating error, though accuracy is a more likely explanation. In this case, the connection was to Oxley's own survey, but people could also connect to other people's work. In this way, they managed to take smaller bits of map and tie them into a map of a larger area, eventually compiling a map of Australia.

In the same way, Stokes wrote of connecting Rottnest Island with the mainland near Fremantle and, by 1860, the inland was filled in to the extent that Wills could be instructed, under certain conditions, 'to turn westward into the country recently discovered by Stuart, and connect his farthest point northward with Gregory's farthest Southern Exploration in 1856 (Mount Wilson)'.

✝

MAKING REFERENCE POINTS

When the ship stopped, there were established survey methods to be used in bays, inlets and rivers as well. James Cook made his name in the Seven Years War, when he charted the St Lawrence Seaway, so Wolfe could land his troops and capture Quebec by scaling the

Heights of Abraham after landing from boats. Before the soldier-filled boats could sneak in under cover of darkness, accurate charts were needed to ensure that the way was safe, and to get the attackers to the right place.

The same style of mapping was exactly what was needed in bays and anchorages. The work would be done from a boat that could be rowed to a position, and held there while bearings and depth measurements were taken, referring back to a base line that had been established on the shore or elsewhere. One such survey, mentioned by Watkin Tench in 1789, was carried out near Sydney.

> A survey of Botany Bay took place in September. I was of the party, with several other officers. We continued nine days in the bay, during which time, the relative position of every part of it, to the extent of more than thirty miles, following the windings of the shore, was ascertained, and laid down on paper, by captain Hunter.

Sometimes, as in the case Tench described, the base line could be measured with ease, at other times, tricks had to be used. James Grant was in Western Port in 1801, and he seems to have used the time difference between a gun's flash and the sound of the shot to measure distances.

> Messrs. Barrallier and Murray went on shore ... in order to the better ascertaining the different points of this harbour that

were in sight; at 8 p.m. fired four guns by the request of Mr.
Barrallier, in order to measure a base line.

With four shots, the land party would presumably have had the
first shot to alert them, and three timing shots that could be
averaged. With bearings from each shore station to the ship and to
the other end of the base line, and with two estimated distances to
the ship, it would then be simple trigonometry to get a measure of
the base line across open water that was within a hundred yards,
near enough to produce a chart of a bay for other ships to rely on.

It worked like this: if you have any two angles of a triangle, you
know that the third will add up to make 180 degrees. If you know
the length of any one side—and they had that by estimating how
long sound took to travel to the shore party at 330 metres per
second—they could calculate the lengths of the other sides. The
secret was that the flash was seen at the moment the gun fired,
and the bang was heard later. It was crude, but good enough for a
first survey.

At other times, explorers would use whatever came to hand. John
Murray, who succeeded Grant on the *Lady Nelson*, used a rope
720 feet (220 metres) long, with floats every 30 feet (9 metres) to
measure a base line on one of the islands of Bass Strait in 1801.

Measured a base line of 324 fathoms in length from one point
of the cove we lay in to the other, it was measured with small
line and every five fathoms of it was a chip of light wood in

length 120 fathoms. We had the boats employed in this business; alternately anchored them till we got across to the southern end of the point of the cove; and as the water was smooth I fancy the length of base line to be correct. I then surveyed the eastern side of the Sound and Cove.

In short, they used a rough floating tape measure to gauge the distance across the bay. By 1819, both the scale and the standards of precision had increased, and Phillip Parker King completed a base line on a beach that was 231 chains in length, almost 5 kilometres. By 1844, Charles Sturt used double that distance as a base line, but still with a degree of dissatisfaction.

The base line was completed on the 19th, and measured six miles. I was anxious to have made it of greater length, but the ground would not admit of it. The angles were necessarily very acute; but the bearings were frequently repeated, and found to agree. I was the less anxious on the point because my intention was to check any error by another line as soon as I could.

When the angles were acute or small, any slight error in measuring the base line or taking the bearing was magnified in calculating distances, so the ideal was to have an angle of at least 30 degrees to the base line in any bearing. A base line needed to be both accurately surveyed and located where it would be most effective, which meant having fixed points that could be seen over a large area of the countryside. In that context, remarkable hills and mountains were ideal.

☩

PERAMBULATORS,
PACE COUNTING AND CHAINS

Lieutenant Dawes may have been an excellent counter of steps taken, but Major Mitchell had chainmen continuously measuring distances covered along his route. Sometimes a simpler measure would do, like the perambulator. This was not for the transport of babies, but a sort of wheelbarrow with a counter attached, a later version of the odometer, which was originally a system of cogged wheels used to measure the length of Roman roads.

A standard adult bicycle has a 28-inch wheel (there is method in my using these old units, as you will see). That converts to a circumference of 88 inches, which means that three rotations cover 22 feet, and nine rotations cover 22 yards, or one chain. A device that counts the rotations of such a wheel will record a mile for every 720 revolutions. If our explorers kept the perambulator going, they could keep track of the distance and direction every 30 minutes or so, and record the details on a traverse board summarizing the day's journey.

Would it matter if a mountaintop 50 miles away were laid down a mile or so out of place? It would matter a great deal because, later on, people who were 50 miles on the other side of that same mountain might use it to connect a second survey. That made scrambling up to the peaks of hills and mountains important. Not only could you see chasms, cliffs and the lie of the land, the way water drained off it, but you could see distant landmarks, drawing them into the triangular grid once more, correcting any systematic errors. Here is John Oxley, in the Warrumbungle Ranges (he called them Arbuthnot's Range) on 8 August 1818:

> We set off early this morning to ascend Mount Exmouth, distant four or five miles: at its base we crossed a pretty stream of water, having its source in the Mount; it took us nearly two hours of hard labour to ascend its rugged summits: we were however amply gratified for our trouble by the extensive prospect we had of the surrounding country. Directing our view to the west, Mount Harris and Mount Forster, whose elevations do not exceed from two to three hundred feet, were distinctly seen at a distance of eighty-nine miles. These two spots excepted, from the south to the north it was a vast level, resembling the ocean in extent and appearance.

From the stream to the top involves an ascent of some 850 metres, hard labour indeed! Some of those bearings were a check on earlier bearings taken from the other prominence. As far back as 20 July, almost three weeks before reaching the Warrumbungles, Oxley was naming the distant peaks and taking them into his notes for later mapping. From Mount Harris, Mount Exmouth was N. 79. E. (that is, 79 degrees east of magnetic north), Mount Harrison was N. 85. E. and Vernon's Peake was at N. 88. E.

Sometimes, the compass could not be trusted. The day before Oxley climbed Mount Exmouth, he walked up the appropriately named Loadstone Hill (Oxley's spelling), where the compass behaved crazily. On the rock, it showed that Mount Exmouth was S. 60. W.—its true bearing is N. 75. E.—but when he raised the compass to eye level, it read N. 67. E. On the rock, 100 metres on, Exmouth was E. 48. S., but at eye level the peak had a bearing of N. 77. E.

A theodolite or a sextant was always better than a compass to measure the angles between objects, but theodolites weighed more and needed heavy tripods to keep them steady, so they were no fun to take up a mountain. The best prismatic compass was only accurate to half a degree or so, good enough for general sketch maps of the landscape, within which tracks, roads, railway lines and telegraphs might be lightly planned, leaving the final path to be chosen by those on the ground.

Such a map would have been excellent value for somebody following later, although most expeditions went out with enough sextants, theodolites, surveyors' chains and other heavy equipment to leave a clear trail that would remain visible years later. Then again, other people had been leaving tracks to follow for many years.

✝

NATIVE ROADS

One thing the first convicts learned while following the trail to Botany Bay was something John Wilson would have known, as would other early runaway convicts: the Aboriginal people had networks of foot tracks all over the country. In the region close to the settlement at Sydney Cove, whites might have assumed any faint pathways they saw were theirs, but to a trained eye the way through the bush became much easier to find.

In wilderness areas, today's bushwalkers still follow tracks that are maintained partly by wildlife and partly by human feet. Few stop to ask whose feet first trod those tracks, as they thread their way across the country, but many explorers wrote of following 'native paths'. That aside, the awareness of these must have come from the convicts who wandered the bush, making the felonry more valuable to the gentry.

The first routes developed as foot tracks, hardly wider than two bare feet side by side. Even today, in the hills of central Australia, pads can be discerned, sliding up the arid hillsides, faint tracks worn into the hills by the feet of countless kangaroos, feral donkeys or other animals. Near Sydney, in the Budawang Ranges—and in other wilderness areas—the ground is criss-crossed with wombat tracks that look for all the world like human walking tracks, until they disappear down a burrow.

Over time, some of these faint traces were taken up by humans; first by the Aborigines and more recently by Europeans. It only takes a few feet walking a track each year to keep it open, especially when the bush is burned regularly so walkers can stay on the track. If the track leads to something useful, like a way up onto a mountain or to water, then more than a few feet will use it each year. Even where a track crosses rocky ground or rock, the scuffing of feet on lichens and mosses leaves a pale trace that can be followed.

In late 1968, I was sent out to check the tracks in Sydney's Royal National Park after severe bushfires had largely wiped out the area. The aim was to see if people were likely to get lost, and whether any signage was needed to mark the tracks, but there was no problem. I found I could see not only the tracks themselves but also occasional branchings where the track had switched at some previous time as walkers avoided an obstacle such as a thorny bush that had sprung up after another fire. I could also see enough glass fragments, from discarded and broken bottles, glittering in the sunlight so that even my untrained eye could see both track edges off into the distance. The tracks needed no signs.

While the Europeans marked the trees as they passed through, so others might follow, the Aborigines did it more subtly. To a trained bush eye, the paths followed by Aborigines in open country in central Australia are marked by bits of discarded stone, flakes from stone tools they shaped as they walked. Most of the explorers had learned to train their eyes, or they had Aboriginal helpers like Wylie and Tommy Winditj along with them, revealing the way forward.

In short, the explorers entered a 'trackless' waste that was, in reality, criss-crossed with everything from minor routes to major highways. All they had to do was follow along, hoping they had made the correct choice. Just as La Pérouse followed an established 'road' to Sydney, so King in 1817 found water in a 'morass' and reported that 'several beaten paths were observed leading to the morass from different directions'. In 1841, Eyre reached 'a well-beaten native road'. The next day he wrote:

> After a little while, we again came to a well beaten native pathway, and following this along the summit of the cliffs, were brought by it, in seven miles, to the point where they receded from the sea-shore; as they inclined inland, leaving a low sandy country between them and some high bare sand-hills near the sea. The road now led us down a very rocky steep part of the cliffs, near the angle where they broke away from the beach, but upon reaching the bottom we lost it altogether on the sandy shore; following along by the water's edge, we felt cooled and refreshed by the sea air, and in one mile and a half from where we had descended the cliffs, we reached the white sand-drifts. Upon turning into these to search for water, we were fortunate enough to strike the very place where the natives had dug little wells ...

In July 1845, Leichhardt noted in his journal that he had seen 'many well beaten footpaths of the natives', and in late August, he wrote '*[f]ollowing* it up, we came to a well beaten foot-path of the natives, which brought us in a short time to a good supply of drinkable, though very brackish water'. In short, the explorers were not really exploring. Rather, they were following marked tracks and mapping them, but they were also learning to read the bush.

✠

EUROPEANS
IN A STRANGE LAND

Outside Yass, Hamilton Hume's old homestead has been preserved. The Australian explorer, revered today as a currency lad, a successful native-born Australian bushman–explorer, had settled down as a farmer there. The site includes a barn, an impressive piece of work with brick ends into which a master bricklayer inserted circular ports, openings for barn owls, which could fly in to prey on mice and rats that might eat the grain stored there. It is an elegant example of the bricklayer's craft. There is just one problem: there are no barn owls in Australia. The openings are appropriate in English barns, but not in Australian ones.

Perhaps the work was done while Hume was away, but this was the same sort of muddled Eurocentric thinking that coloured many explorers' plans, assumptions and actions. The good ones, though, had common sense. Thomas Mitchell may have had little sympathy with the land but he watched the lay of the land with a soldier's eye, the way it sloped and drained. Because of this, he could head away from the Gwydir River, yet know, when it later joined the Darling, that this river could, from its position and size, only be the Gwydir.

Augustus Gregory and his brothers were born in Britain, but they came to Australia as boys, and they were all superb bushmen. Sturt and Eyre arrived as adults with European eyes, yet they seem to have acquired a real sense for the land. The German-born Leichhardt arrived at the Gulf of Carpentaria with no idea that there were crocodiles in the area. Leichhardt was sneered at by Mitchell and his cronies because he set out to live off the land, but Leichhardt's work was far cheaper than that of the egotistical major, who needed a huge supply of stores and equipment to keep going because he treated each excursion as a military campaign.

As explorers became more confident in the Australian bush and more familiar with the land, they began using other clues for navigation. By 1817, Allan Cunningham was deducing his position from the plant species he saw, though two days later John Oxley expressed his doubts about this method in his own journal:

> The plants on the banks and in the stream were precisely similar to those on the Macquarie in the vicinity of Bathurst; but I have observed that no certain conclusions can be drawn from a similarity between the botanical productions of two places, a truth which has been exemplified more than once in the course of this Journal.

Two years later, Oxley was more inclined to use this trick, noting that a banksia had appeared when they were in the same meridian as the Macquarie River, where it was also found. He speculated that 'particular productions of the vegetable as well as of the mineral kingdom run in veins nearly north and south through the country', adding that this was apparent in a number of plants.

✝

THE MAN WHO
COULD NOT SPELL

The first person sent over the Blue Mountains to make maps was George Evans, a man who quickly understood the country. Reading between the lines, he was a man you would like to have as a grandfather. He was decent, competent, expert even in finding his way across an alien landscape, but he had one failing that did not impress his shallow masters in Whitehall: he could not spell. When in 1813 he was sent in the footsteps of Blaxland, Wentworth and Lawson, with instructions to go beyond, right over the mountains, to survey the land on the far side, the rivulet he crossed became the River Lett when his report was transcribed!

To the South of me there are large hills much higher than the one I am on, with pasture to their tops; This Range is rather overrun with underwood and larger Timber growing thereon, but the sides are as green as possible; in descending for 2 Miles the verdure is good; the descent then becomes steep for a $^1/_4$ of a Mile, leading into a fine valley at the end I met a large Riverlett arising from the Southern Hills. We shot Ducks and caught several trout weighing at least 5 or 6 Pounds each.

This spelling irregularity did not impress the aristocratic Henry, Earl of Bathurst, even though Evans had named the Bathurst Plains after him, so George Evans, who even spent Christmas Day 1813 on duty, just had to be let go (or was he lett go?). Here is his Christmas Day diary:

Being Christmas day we remained for a day's rest; yet we walked about as much as a day's journey looking around us, and ascending Hills to see the Country, which is excellent pasture, the soil is light, but exceeds the Forest Lands in general on the East side of the Mountains. The day is so hott the Fish will not bite; it is the only time they have missed; therefore I opened my tin case of Roasted Beef.

Before the relegation blow could fall, George had one more trip on his own, when he found the Lachlan River (which was named, by the way, not after Governor Lachlan Macquarie, but after his son, Lachlan junior). Macquarie, however, was too good a judge of human capability to lose Evans entirely, and if he could not send Evans out on his own, he could certainly send him out with Oxley, who benefited greatly from being accompanied by a man who could work independently. Having an experienced hand like Evans along meant people who were new to the exploring game could benefit from his knowledge, especially when it came to deciding what to take.

Selecting what to pack was, after all, always going to be a desperate compromise.

✝

5.

Packing
to go

SUPPOSE YOU WERE GOING OUT for a couple of months in what is, to you, a total wilderness. Everything you need to wear, everything you need to eat, drink and use must either be carried, or you must carry the equipment to make it or catch it or find it. You need instruments to measure where you are, you need books and paper to record where you have been, you need weapons so you can defend yourself and kill game, ammunition, repair kits, tools, small goods to give to friendly natives, and that is the bare minimum. Most of the exploration parties took a great deal more.

Explorers in the earliest days had to make do with whatever they could find or borrow. Over time, 'tricks of the trade' developed and were passed on to others. Planning became an art, but the final choice was always a trade-off, and if somebody made a bad choice, somebody would die.

Throughout this time, the equipment used on land voyages was less than ideal. Even 50 years into the exploration of Australia by land, John Lort Stokes still wrote of 'fashioning slings' before some of the crew of the *Beagle* set off to make a long trek in from the coast of northern Australia, but they knew what to take by then. Half a century before Stokes, the thoughts of men heading into the bush must have been filled with fears: *do we have the right things?*

There were ways to cut down on what was required. No Australian explorer seems to have thought of it, but in America in 1804, Meriwether Lewis and William Clark needed to keep their powder dry as they set out to reach the Pacific coast, partly by boat. They carried their gunpowder in lead containers made of just enough lead to melt down and make the number of bullets the powder would shoot from the guns.

Perhaps the Australians were not sufficiently worried about any excess of water in central Australia. They did, however, need to carry powder and shot safely in containers that were safe from shredding thorns and, to a certain extent, waterproofed from rain, water carried, or water encountered in river crossings.

Then there was the question of how everything was carried. A cart or dray would be able to carry more than the horse(s) pulling it could carry in saddle bags, but wheeled vehicles caused problems at cliffs and narrow passes, while thick scrub needed clearing to get wagons through, which meant the explorers would need more axes. So perhaps saddle bags would be better, but saddle bags would rip on thick scrub and thorns, meaning the explorers would in turn need spare canvas, needles and thread ... every choice had its cost.

The international tourist today has a baggage allowance of 20 kilograms, and carries perhaps another 10 kilograms in hand luggage. With a well-made rucksack, a fit walker can carry 20 kilograms comfortably, and 30 kilograms at a pinch—but be prepared to be tired if you are carrying at the top end of the scale over rough ground. The tourist can buy missing and lost items in shops, food and drink will be available, and shelter and bedding will be provided by friendly hotels. The explorer can make no such assumptions. Any lost or broken item, anything left behind, must either be done without or replaced with something made on the spot.

The only way to get beyond a 30-kilogram limit is to use a boat, a ship, a wheeled vehicle, or beasts of burden. Ships and boats need stores of their own and cannot go overland very well, wheeled vehicles are hard to get over rough ground or through thick scrub and forest, and even beasts of burden need stores such as horseshoes, harnesses and saddles. The animals also need extra medicines.

The under-equipped or careless tourist risks at worst a slightly spoiled holiday, at least until a replacement is found for the essential but lost or damaged item. The explorer, on the other hand, risks death if an alternative cannot be found or made. That means there is a perilous line to tread between, on the one hand, taking too much and perishing and, on the other hand, taking too little and perishing.

✢

THE OVERLOADERS

As they left Melbourne to find a route from there to the north coast
for the telegraph line, the Victorian Exploring Expedition (VEE)
was widely criticized for taking excessive material, which was fair
enough. The odd thing was that they were compared at the time
with Herschel Babbage, who may have taken large amounts of
equipment, but who knew, unlike Burke, what he was doing.

Benjamin Herschel Babbage, to give him his full name, was the
clever son of the ingenious Charles Babbage, the computer pioneer
who designed the difference engine that was to create error-free
mathematical tables for navigators everywhere to use. Herschel
Babbage was a man of science who had worked with his father on
the difference engine and with the renowned engineer Isambard
Kingdom Brunel on railway projects in Europe. Such a man might
be thought an odd choice to be an explorer, but Babbage was widely
read in the sciences, as you would expect of somebody whose usual
given name commemorated his father's friend, John Herschel, a
member of an eminent astronomical dynasty. Among his valued
skills, Babbage was a good geologist, and the government of the
colony of South Australia was just starting to realize it had mineral
resources that needed to be identified so they could be exploited.
They chose Herschel Babbage to do it for them.

Babbage does not seem to have had much access to other explorers, so he had to work things out from logical first principles and, like any competent scientist of his era, he engaged in over-engineering, treating safety as paramount. His original bills and receipts have been preserved, so it is possible to see what this man of science took with him when he headed for the desert. As an engineer, rather than as a surveyor, he planned meticulously, knowing the sort of country he was going into. He thought scientifically and identified the problems he might encounter.

In this he was unlike Adelaide's citizens, equally recent arrivals from England, with no knowledge of the land, and no patience with those who did not immediately make them rich. Babbage's analytical mind and careful planning made no sense to the vociferous, pugnacious and unqualified critics of his equipment, but Babbage was headed for a long, slow, thorough haul that would find what was there to be found, free of error.

His was the sensible engineering solution, but you have to suspect that, like a lot of engineers, Babbage may have been less skilled at understanding his fellow humans. These grasping and rapacious people wanted to hear only of lands of milk and honey, or by then, even better, a local El Dorado that would attract back some of the colony's labourers who were rushing off to the diggings of New South Wales and Victoria. Slow, safe and methodical be hanged—they wanted quick results!

Babbage's financial accounts reflect a man who knew what was needed, and got it. He paid for an inspection of the horses before he bought them, he acquired a kangaroo dog, bought pistols, medicines, the published journals of Leichhardt and Grey, a nautical almanac and two books on home medicine. At a time when many people lived isolated lives, there was a ready supply of DIY medical works in Australia.

He also bought instruments for collecting botanical specimens, a cedar box and presses, chemicals, bags, nets, entomological pins, a 'lupe' (a loupe, or hand lens), one pound weight of quicksilver, plant presses, compasses, drawing books, colours and pencils, stationery, tents, dray covers, hay, oats, a cart whip, forage, wadding, more pistols and caps, 60 pounds of lead, a rocket mould fitted with brass for £6.7.6, picks, American tomahawks and other tools, including a spokeshave, plane, chisels and augers, footbaths, candles, lanterns, 7 pounds of mustard, 6 pounds of garlic … and on and on.

It was a planned and calculated expedition that would take samples, keep them secure, and bring them back; an expedition that would take men out into new (to them) territory and bring them back as well. However, one of the items, the rocket mould, stands out as odd. Many expeditions used rockets for signalling purposes, and off northern Australia the crew of the *Beagle* used a Congreve rocket to frighten off warriors without drawing blood when trouble appeared to be brewing. Babbage probably realized that if he needed rockets, he could convert ordinary gunpowder by adding some charcoal and maybe some sulfur from the medicine chest, so as to reduce the saltpetre content from 75 per cent to the 60 per cent that is needed to make good rocket powder.

Some of these items, like the footbaths, might seem a little unusual, but consider the conditions his men would be walking in. The baths would also have doubled as containers for small items, or water containers if it rained. Babbage was heading out onto open plains where the slopes would be gentle, where there would be no jungle, no ravines to get past. So why did Babbage get bad press? It all came down to politics, and Babbage lost out to the machinations of Peter Warburton, who was sent out by the anxious citizens of Adelaide to take over from him.

Thanks largely to Warburton's later comments, and the comments of his friends at the Royal Geographic Society, Babbage's work was treated as worthless, but he had inspected and mapped the area around modern Woomera quite thoroughly, and had even found a way through Eyre's 'horseshoe lake'. It isn't enough to collect data and bring it back: you need to persuade people to listen, and Babbage seems never to have cared enough to do that.

Burke and George Landells (Wills was yet to become second-in-command) of the VEE were the classic overloaders. On the way up to Swan Hill, their wagons often sank to their axles in the mud, so some of the goods were auctioned off. At Swan Hill, three-quarters of a ton of sugar, large amounts of lime juice and three tents were disposed of, but given that all of the four who made it to the continent's northern shore were probably victims of scurvy, this was not a good idea. Even if the lime juice had only made it to Menindie or Cooper's Creek, it would have delayed the scurvy, which also struck the party waiting at the depot known as the DIG tree, forcing them to retreat just as Burke, Wills and King were almost there. Babbage would have known better. Wills should have done.

✝

CARNEGIE'S LIST

David Carnegie left us a complete account of what he took on a prospecting expedition, at the end of a century of expeditions. If he strikes us as one of the more obnoxious explorers, this may be a result of his meticulous account of his activities, even when they reflected badly on him, as we regard him with modern eyes.

I subjoin a list of the articles and provisions with which we started: —

- 8 pack-camels. Bulls. South Australian bred. Of ages varying from five to fifteen years. 1 riding-camel. Bull. S.A. bred. Age five years. Average value of camels; 72 pounds 10 shillings each.
- 8 pack saddles of Afghan make, 1 riding saddle, made to order by Hardwick, Coolgardie, specially light, and stuffed with chaff, A very excellent saddle, 1 camel brand, D.W.C, 1 doz. nose pegs.
- 6 coils of clothes line, 3 coils of wallaby line [like window-blind cord] for nose lines, 5 hanks of twine, 2 long iron needles for saddle mending [also used as cleaning-rod for guns], 2 iron packers for arranging stuffing of saddle. Spare canvas. Spare

calico. Spare collar-check. Spare leather, for hobbles and neck-straps. Spare buckles for same. Spare bells. Spare hobble-chains. 6 lbs. of sulphur, 2 gallons kerosene, to check vermin in camels, 2 gallons tar and oil, for mange in camels.

■   2 galvanized-iron water casks [15 gallons each], 2 galvanized-iron water casks [17 gallons each], made with bung on top side, without taps, for these are easily broken off, 1 India-rubber pipe for drawing water from tanks, 1 funnel, 3 three-gallon buckets, 1 tin canteen [2 gallons], 2 canvas water tanks, to be erected on poles to hold water baled from soak, &c, 4 canvas water-bags [10 gallons each.] 4 canvas water-bags [1½ gallons each] slung on camels' necks.

■   6 Ballarat picks and handles, 3 shovels, 1 axe [7 lbs.], 1 hammer [7 lbs.], 1 engineer's hammer, 3 tomahawks, 1 saw, 1 small flat iron anvil, 1 small pair of bellows, 1 iron windlass-handle and fittings, 1 1-inch chisel, 1 brace and bits, 1¾ inch auger bit, 1 emery stone, 4 iron dishes, 1 sieve-dish, 1 iron dolly, 1 soldering iron for mending water casks, 2 sticks solder for mending water casks, 1 bottle spirits of salts for mending water casks, 1 case of tools, Screwdriver, small saw, hammer, chisel, file, gimlet, leather-punch, wire nipper, screw wrench, large scissors, &c, 1 case of tools for canvas work [sewing needles, &c.], 2 lbs. of copper rivets. Screws. Bolts. 1 box copper wire. Strong thread. 1½ lbs. 3-inch nails. 1 lb. 2-inch nails.

■   50 feet of rope, 1 duck tent, 6 ft, x 8 ft, 4 flies, 10 ft, x 12 ft., for covering packs, 4 mosquito nets, 3 saucepans, 3 quart pots,

6 pannikins, 6 plates, enamelled tin, 6 knives, forks, and spoons,
1 stewpan, 1 frying pan, 1 small medicine case [in tabloid form],
7 lbs. Epsom salts, 6 bottles of Elliman's embrocation, 3 bottles
of carbolic oil, 3 bottles of eye lotion, 3 bottles of eucalyptus oil.
2 galvanized-iron concertina-made boxes for perishable goods,
e.g., ammunition, journals, &c, 2 twelve-bore shot-guns, 4 colt
revolvers, .380 calibre, 4 Winchester repeaters, .44 calibre,
200 twelve-bore cartridges, 300 Winchester ditto, 200 revolver
ditto.

■ 1 bicycle lamp [for night observations], 1 5-inch theodolite and
tripod, 2 prismatic compasses, 2 steering compasses [Gregory's
pattern], 1 telescope, 1 pair field-glasses, 1 map case, 1 drawing-
board. Drawing materials, note-books, &c. 1 binocular camera,
with films, [N.B. Not good in hot climate.] 1 tape measure.

■ 14 50-lb. bags of flour [700 lbs.], 35 doz. 1-lb, tins of meat
[420 lbs.], 5 doz. 1-lb. tins of fish [60 lbs.], [N.B. — Not fit for
consumption — thrown away.] 200 lbs. rice, 70 lbs. oatmeal,
6 doz. tins of milk [condensed], 8 doz. tins baking powder,
4 doz. 1-lb tins of jam, 140 lbs. sugar, 40 lbs. salt [for salting
down meat — kangaroo, &c.], 30 lbs. tea, 2 doz. tinned fruit,
2 doz. tinned vegetables, 10 lbs. currants, 10 lbs. raisins, 40 lbs.
dried apricots, 6 doz. 1-lb. tins butter, 4 doz. Liebig's Extract,
1^1/$_2$ doz. pepper [^{1}/$_4$-lb. tins], ^{1}/$_2$ doz. curry-powder [^{1}/$_4$-lb. tins],
9 packets Sunlight soap, 1 box of candles, 6 lbs. cornflour,
28 doz. matches, 50 lbs. tobacco, 100 lbs. preserved potatoes.

■ 4 bottles good brandy, 1 bottle good rum, 1 hair clipper, blankets,

boots, flannel shirts, trousers [Dungaree and moleskin];
&c.

As well as listing all of these goods, Carnegie knew he was writing largely for a 'home' (that is, British) audience who might perhaps have seen a camel exhibited in a zoo or a circus, but who would never have seen one laden. He continued, explaining some of the choices in detail:

The stores were calculated to last six months with care and longer should we encounter good country where game could be shot. Everything that could be was packed in large leather bags, made to order. Other expeditions have carried wooden brass-bound boxes; I do not approve of these—first on account of their own weight and bulk; second, when empty they are equally bulky and awkward; third, unless articles are of certain shapes and dimensions they cannot be packed in the boxes, which do not 'give' like bags. Wooden water casks are generally used—my objections to them are that they weigh more than the iron ones, are harder to mend, and when empty are liable to spring or warp from the hot sun.

It will be seen that a great part of our load consisted of tools which, though weighty, were necessary, should we come on auriferous country, or be forced to sink to any depth for water: a great many of these tools were left in the desert.

The average load with which each camel started, counting the water casks [the four large ones] full, was 531 lbs., exclusive of saddle. Kruger and Shiddi carried over 750 lbs. including top loading and saddle.

These loads, though excessive had the season been summer, were not too great to start with in the cooler weather; and every day made some difference in their weight.

Carnegie could take a heavy load because he had excellent camels, and people who knew how to manage them. It took time for people to realize that camels were more than misshapen committee-designed horses, all the jaded European eye could see.

☩

BEASTS OF BURDEN

In the earliest days, as the first colonial explorers poked around in the bush, they had no choice but to carry things themselves. Later, horses and bullocks were used to carry equipment, but there were many who had other ideas about how to solve the problem.

As early as 1806, Matthew Flinders wanted to make a dash for the centre of the continent, starting from either the bottom of the Gulf of Carpentaria with 'five or six asses to carry provisions (and they can be obtained here)', or else 'from the head of the great gulph on the south coast in 32 deg'. In August 1841 John Lort Stokes was in the Gulf of Carpentaria, not far from where Burke and Wills reached the coast, and writing from the *Beagle*, suggested using camels:

> My position was in latitude 17 degrees 58^1/$_2$ minutes South longitude 7 degrees 12^1/$_2$ East of Port Essington, or 139 degrees 25 minutes East of Greenwich; and within four hundred miles from the centre of the continent. What an admirable point of departure for exploring the interior! A few camels, with skins for conveying water, would be the means of effecting this great end in a very short time. In one month these ships of the desert, as they have been appropriately called, might accomplish, at a trifling expense, that which has been attempted in vain by the outlay of so much money. When we consider that Australia is our own continent, and that now, after sixty years of occupation, we are in total ignorance of the interior, though thousands are annually spent in geographical research, it seems not unreasonable to expect that so important a question should at length be set at rest.

With Harry's death, Australia became free of camels, but more trials with them were inevitable. In 1860, some camels were imported from India for the Burke and Wills expedition, and by 1866 Sir Thomas Elder had established a camel stud at Beltana in the dry north of South Australia. Within a few years,

Ernest Giles proved just how effective the animals could be. Soon 'Afghans' (mainly from an area that is now part of Pakistan) were flooding into Australia and running huge trains of camels across the dry inland. Now camels are accounted a feral pest— but in the nineteenth century they served Australian exploration remarkably well. Giles, one of the best of the desert explorers in Australia, wrote:

> My first and second expeditions were conducted entirely with horses; in all my after journeys I had the services of camels, those wonderful ships of the desert, without whose aid the travels and adventures which are subsequently recorded could not possibly have been achieved, nor should I now be alive, as Byron says, to write so poor a tale, this lowly lay of mine.

Giles made his five journeys in the period 1872 to 1876; keep 1876 in mind for a moment. In 1922, Bessie Threadgill wrote her fine history of land exploration in South Australia in the period 1856 to 1880. She relied heavily on written sources, but must have talked either to some of the old explorers or to those who had known them, making her asides and chapter endings a good indication of the realities of mapping a parched landscape. At the end of chapter VI, she wrote, 'In 1870 camels for Australian exploration were exotics, worth travelling many miles to see, and not always recognized when seen. In 1876, they were more indispensable than damper, bully beef or blackfellow.'

Perhaps we can let that non-PC term stand for now. It was normal usage in her time and reminds us of an important truth that we have already visited: without their Aboriginal companions, explorers were nothing. Camels were worth even more than experienced guides or basic food, because camels could travel long distances without water and carry tremendous loads, but Threadgill was writing of a later period and so did not mention Horrocks' sad fate.

In September 1844, Leichhardt exchanged a broken cart that would have been of little use to him for three good travelling bullocks, and trained five draught bullocks for the pack-saddle. He said that he and his companions had little knowledge of the animals, but the bullocks survived and Leichhardt came to regard them as extremely useful, even if they slowed the party's progress on the way to Port Essington. They were good to carry 150 pounds (68 kilograms) each, he said.

Slowly, routes began to be laid down, some of them taking travellers from one agricultural area to another, while the more daring and skilful explorers ventured out into unknown territory, ranging in search of new agricultural land. The explorers now generally knew what they were about, though they still had little idea of the hellish country for which they were headed. Still, they began to recognize in the 1860s that camels were far better suited to travel across the parched interior than horses.

While long-necked camels can snatch bites to eat as they stride along, horses and bullocks must stop to feed, and even camels need to fill up on food at the end of the day. All beasts of burden need to be turned loose when they are unloaded, so they can refuel. This relative freedom caused a variety of problems. Bullocks would stubbornly turn around and try to go back the way they came, horses would start at some noise and gallop off, long-legged camels might also stride off, as fast as a man could walk, or gallop a great deal faster than a man could run.

In the morning, one or two of the more accomplished bushmen would need to go out, track the animals, and bring them back into the camp. The task could be made easier by hobbling the animals, strapping the two front legs fairly close together, allowing them slow movement but no more. In open country, another trick was to go out and climb a hill or a tree as dusk closed in to see which way the animals had headed, and to assess what they were feeding on and how much feed there was.

Clever horses can move quite fast in hobbles by rearing slightly and moving the front feet together, and even hobbled camels can wander quite a distance during the night, so the explorers' journals are full of complaints that the day began late as the animals had wandered. A good bushman, able to sense where the animals would be and able to track them, was a valuable member of the party, but much of that reputation for sensing the animals' whereabouts came from knowledge of their habits and preferences, and observing their behaviour, in particular if they had found good feed and, if not, the direction in which they were headed.

✢

BOATS, CANTED HORSES AND DROWNED SHEEP

Early exploration around Sydney used boats to transport heavy equipment and people to a convenient starting place. In 1790, Arthur Phillip rowed and sailed up the Hawkesbury River, trying to reach what were then the Carmarthen Ranges, soon to be called 'the Blue Mountains'.

A number of explorers in the 1830s and 1840s had sea support, from the *Waterwitch* and *Hero* used by Eyre, to the *Beagle* supporting George Grey on the coast of Western Australia, and the *Rattlesnake* and other vessels supporting Edmund Kennedy on his ill-fated Cape York jaunt.

Augustus Gregory used horses with pack-saddles only, which somewhat annoyed Charles Sturt who was advising him, but Gregory was able to cross from Roma in Queensland to Adelaide along the Cooper and Strzelecki creeks in less than three months in 1858—and in the process, prove that there was no 'horseshoe lake' barrier to Adelaide's north, as Eyre and others had believed, and Babbage had already disproved in 1856. The only drawback with horses was the water they needed.

In 1855, Gregory had used a small schooner, the *Tom Tough*, and the barque *Monarch*. He was to explore the Victoria River, previously visited by Captain Stokes some fourteen years earlier. The naval party took boats up the river as far as they could go, but without horses and suitable equipment there was a limit to their progress.

The *Tom Tough* was crammed to the gunwales with horses to ride and carry things, sheep to eat, drays, blacksmith's tools, powder, shot, guns, saddles, saddlebags, waterbags, tents and much more— though some of this would be left at their shore base, where they would return from time to time.

All the same, they took a fair amount with them, and on one trip in January 1856 Gregory lists the supplies taken for a party of nine men. He had 27 packhorses with pack-saddles, six riding horses, and three more packhorses with riding saddles. Their load:

> Provisions for five months: Flour, 1,470 pounds; pork, 1200 pounds; rice, 200 pounds; sago, 44 pounds; sugar, 280 pounds; tea, 36 pounds; coffee, 28 pounds; tobacco, 21 pounds; soap, 51 pounds. Total, 3,330 pounds.
>
> Equipment: Instruments, clothing, tents, ammunition, horseshoes, tools, etc., 800 pounds; saddle-bags and packages, 400 pounds; saddles, bridles, hobbles, etc., 900 pounds. Total, 5,430 pounds.

At one time, the *Monarch* spent two weeks high and dry and canted over on a reef, to the immense discomfort of the horses she was carrying—and the sheep were not particularly happy about living in a sloping hold for two weeks either. Later, the *Tom Tough* was seriously damaged after she ran onto rocks while working up a river, to the extent that the hold partly filled with water, spoiling some of the food.

One of the ship's boats was leaky, and being left unbailed one night, she sank, drowning eleven sheep, which had presumably been left in there to save them from the 'alligators'—the crocodiles had already killed a kangaroo dog and tried to attack some of the horses. Still, the schooner had enough tools, so the crew cut logs and made timbers so she could be repaired and sail off to Timor for more stores. She also carried a 'portable boat', a primitive inflatable made of fabric coated with India rubber, but the rubber perished, so the boat proved less useful than they had hoped.

The effective mapping of coasts and possible harbours meant taking small boats and tiny ships close inshore. They might be unstable platforms for star and sun sights, and they were easily buffeted by the waves, but in a tight situation a small cutter was easier to manoeuvre and small boats could skip over shallows that would rip the bottom out of a larger vessel. Still, small craft were unsuitable for long voyages, even if Bass and Flinders had managed well in an extremely small boat. On at least one occasion, they were very lucky to avoid being swamped in a storm.

The usual solution was to combine a smaller vessel and a larger one. The smaller craft came close-in, taking soundings in likely anchorages, searching for places where ships might take on water, and taking a detailed look at coastal features. Lieutenant King was inclined to criticize the work of his French predecessors, but he made it clear from time to time that he had a smaller craft which could get closer to the shore and see a cape where somebody had reported an island, or vice versa. Then again, instruments and other equipment were slowly improving as well, so the task became easier.

Kennedy's expedition to Cape York landed 28 horses, 100 sheep, three kangaroo dogs, and one sheep dog at their starting place. In fact, when you look into it, it seems that dogs were very popular as companions, all the way back to Cook and Banks, who had a greyhound.

George Evans was accompanied by dogs that ran down and killed a kangaroo, while Cunningham reported that his dogs had caught and killed both emus and kangaroos. The emu, he said, just needed some young *Rhagodia* leaves to make an excellent supper. The dogs also served to sound the alarm whenever Aborigines approached.

As he prepared to leave for Western Australia, Eyre sent his dray ahead, and:

... rode with Mr. Scott up to Mr. White's station to wish him good bye, and to make another effort to secure an additional dog or two; finding that he would not sell the noble mastiff I so much wished to have, I bought from him two good kangaroo dogs, at rather a high price, with which I hastened on after the drays, and soon overtook them, but not before my new dogs had secured two fine kangaroos.

Sturt's dogs also caught food, and even specimens, but the explorer complained that one specimen of 'the Dipus of Mitchell', a hopping-mouse, *Notomys mitchelli*, had been so mangled that it was not worth preserving. Sometimes the animals won. Leichhardt mentioned an old man kangaroo that 'took refuge in a water-hole, where it was killed, but at the expense of two of our kangaroo dogs, which were mortally wounded'.

Leichhardt's last kangaroo dog died late in their expedition, but their terrier, which had been brought along as a pet and watch dog, died of heat exhaustion much earlier. Leichhardt commented:

During summer, the ground is so hot, and frequently so rotten, that even the feet of a dog sink deep. This heat, should there be a want of water during a long stage, and perhaps a run after game in addition, would inevitably kill a soft dog. It is, therefore, of the greatest importance to have a good traveller, with hard feet: a cross of the kangaroo dog with the bloodhound would be, perhaps, the best. He should be light, and satisfied with little food in case of scarcity; although the dried tripe of our bullocks gave ample and good food to one dog. It is necessary to carry water for them; and to a little calabash, which we obtained from the natives of the Isaacs, we have been frequently indebted for the life of Spring.

Both Stuart and Gibson had dogs called Toby. Stuart's Toby died of the heat; Gibson's dog wandered off into the desert while both Giles and Gibson were ill and was never found.

Probably no dog would have been as useful as the hypothetical one based on an invention credited to Sir Kenelm Digby. His father was involved in Guy Fawkes' Gunpowder Plot, but the son was only two years old and suffered no taint. As a naval commander, he understood the need for portable time, but as he died in 1665, long before somebody put forward the invention I am about to describe, he ought to escape any taint once again.

Digby developed 'a sympathetic powder' for the cure of wounds. This powder was to be put on the weapon that caused the wound, not the wound itself. He claimed that when a dressing from a wound was placed in a basin of the powder, the person jumped.

In 1687, an anonymous inventor proposed that each ship putting to sea be provided with a scientifically wounded dog, which was to travel on the ship while the dressing remained in the home port. Each hour, day and night, some careful person in the home port would take a dressing that had been on the wounded dog, and place it in Digby's sympathetic powder. This would cause the dog to yelp, thereby indicating for those on the ship the time back in the home port. It gives a whole new meaning to the watchdog or, at sea, to the dog watches.

Sadly, the sympathetic powder time system never worked, so explorers needed to load up with sextants, chronometers, barometers, thermometers and more—and use them a good deal.

6.

Essential instruments and unwanted items

You can't get back home if you don't know where you are; and if you don't know where you are and don't have a map, you can't go back there again. Every explorer needed to know how to navigate, and needed to take along navigational instruments.

To measure longitude, navigators need accurate time. With a reliable chronometer, they watch the sun and the time of local noon and compare that with a clock keeping Greenwich time. If noon comes an hour early, they are 15 degrees east of Greenwich, 64 minutes early means 16 degrees, a difference of 65 minutes is 16°15', and so on. The bottom line is that if a timepiece is out by four minutes—and in a long voyage, that is not at all unlikely—they are faced with a distance error of up to 60 nautical miles or 100 kilometres (at the equator, rather less to the north or south).

Sailing towards the western coast of Australia at night, an error of just a few kilometres can mean disaster.

Determining latitude just requires using an instrument to measure the angle between the horizon and a given celestial body or bodies, and looking up a table to find what the angle would be at the equator at the same time. The difference in degrees is the latitude, and while that is complex, it is nothing when compared with the challenge of computing longitude.

A single sighting, the altitude of one celestial body, does not determine a position, but it yields a circular path large enough to let us treat the local section as a straight line. A second sighting yields a second intersecting line, locating the position; and ideally, a third sighting confirms the position by passing through the same point on the map.

On open water or in desert areas, night and morning sneak up gradually. In the Royal Navy, daylight is when you can see a grey goose at a mile. In Islam, day is heralded by the muezzin's call to prayer as soon as a black thread and a white thread can be distinguished at arm's length. In a river valley, with overhanging trees, it gets dark sooner, often before the sky itself is dark enough to reveal the target stars or planets. So the artificial horizon was a boon to the explorer who could not see a clear horizon. It was generally a container of mercury, but Augustus Gregory sometimes used a pannikin of tea to get a good horizontal surface.

Taking sights could be worrying, as Stokes explained after one of his trips ashore in northern Australia, extending the coastal map.

I got the requisite observation for latitude during the night; and since necessity is ever the mother of invention, read off my sextant by a torch made for the occasion from pieces of paperbark. It will easily be believed, that I did not needlessly prolong the work; for the light of the torch rendered me a prominent mark for any prowling savage to hurl his spear at ...

In some ways, friendly Aborigines in the area may have been a greater problem for navigators than hostile ones, as Eyre discovered in September 1840, just north of Mount Arden in South Australia, when some of his equipment quietly evaporated. His account also offers some insights into how he took his sights.

I occupied myself in writing and charting during the day, and at night amused myself in taking stellar observations for latitude. I had already taken the altitude of Vega, and deduced the latitude to be 32 degrees 3 minutes 23 seconds S.; leaving my artificial horizon on the ground outside whilst I remained in the tent waiting until Altair came to the meridian, I then took my sextant and went out to observe this star also; but upon putting down my hand to take hold of the horizon glass in order to wipe the dew off, my fingers went into the quicksilver—the horizon glass was gone, and also the piece of canvass I had put on the ground to lie down upon whilst observing so low an altitude as that of Vega. Searching a little more I missed a spade, a parcel of horse shoes, an axe, a tin dish, some ropes, a grubbing hoe, and several smaller things which had been left outside the tent, as not being likely to take any injury from the damp.

Precision instruments need careful handling. Near the Peake River in central Australia, Stuart was dismayed to find that when the horse carrying the instruments broke away it burst the girths and threw the saddlebags on the ground. 'The instruments were very much injured, in fact very nearly ruined; the sextant being put out of adjustment, has taken me all day to repair, and I am not sure now whether it is correct or not. It is a great misfortune,' he wrote in his journal. Oxley had a similar problem in 1818 when his chronometer stopped after a severe shaking, but the real annoyance was that his government-supplied watch also stopped.

LUNARS
AND ECLIPSES

Scientists around the Mediterranean had long known that lunar eclipses reached totality in different parts of the sky and at different local times. Then they saw that if angle measures could be taken on the moon at the moment that it was first all in shadow, the relative longitudes of the observation sites might be closely compared.

Lunar eclipses are rare, and so useless to navigators. Solar eclipses, equally uncommon, may be missed behind clouds and vary widely as the narrow path of totality travels across the planet. But some eclipses happen all the time, as regular as clockwork, when the moons of Jupiter go around that planet. As the moon moves behind the planet, that is an immersion, and as it comes back out again, that is an emersion.

There are six points in the motion of a Jovian moon that can be observed and timed: when the moon appears to be one lunar diameter from Jupiter; when it is just touching Jupiter; when it has just disappeared behind the planet; when the first edge of it appears from behind; when it appears to be just touching; and when it is one diameter from Jupiter again.

Given the sizes of the bodies involved, the views from opposite sides of Earth are slightly different but still almost simultaneous, so the moons of Jupiter behave much like a distant clock that everybody can see. So why wasn't this method of determining relative longitude used more often?

The snag was that the observer needed a telescope to see the four main moons, and on a ship the telescope cannot stay accurately trained on the planet. Galileo Galilei designed a telescope mounted on a helmet that an observer could wear while sitting on a gimballed chair (a seat designed to remain level even as the ship pitched and rolled—it could do nothing about yaw, where the ship changes direction). It was about as useful as Kenelm Digby's dog, and never went to sea.

Observing the eclipses of the moons of Jupiter was impractical on a heaving deck at night, with sails, masts and rigging getting in the way, but on land these eclipses were an available tool, so long as somebody had the right tables showing the expected time of a moon's eclipse. Then you just had to be watching at the right time, though that was often a problem thanks to cloud cover.

James Cook used the method at least once. His report, dated 29 June 1770, was written when he was ashore at Endeavour River, in a much easier environment for astronomy than any found at sea.

> This night Mr. Green and I observ'd an Emersion of Jupiter's first Satellite, which hapned at 2 hours 58 minutes 53 seconds in the A.M.; the same Emersion hapnd at Greenwich, according to Calculation, on the 30th at 5 hours 17 minutes 43 seconds A.M. The differance is 14 hours 18 minutes 50 seconds, equal to 214 degrees 42 minutes 30 seconds of Longitude, which this place is West of Greenwich, and its Latitude 15 degrees 26 minutes South.

On 17 July, a second measure yielded a difference of '14 hours 19 minutes 35 seconds equal to 214 degrees 53 minutes 45 seconds of Longitude'. Averaging the two, Cook obtained a longitude of 214 degrees 48 minutes 7$\frac{1}{2}$ seconds west or, in modern terms, 145°11'52.5" east, compared with the modern value for Cooktown of 145°16' east, an error of about 4 nautical miles (7.5 kilometres), some of which may be explained if Cook observed at some point inland from the centre of the modern township.

Others to use Jovian moons were Charles Sturt and John Wills, but there was another method: the use of 'lunars' or 'lunar distances'. These rely on the way the moon orbits Earth about once every 30 days, so each day it changes its place in the sky by about 12 degrees: that is half a degree, one lunar width, as we see it from Earth, each hour. This means the moon is seen to be moving constantly across the 'fixed' stars and also the sun. More importantly, it will be seen in a particular position with respect to a star at the same time, whether you are looking from Greenwich or central Australia.

This means that if the relative positions of the moon and the sun, or of the moon and some other star, can be measured, this angle can be related to a particular clock time at the reference point (generally Greenwich). You simply have to set your clock by the sun at noon then note the local time at which the moon reaches that position, and you have an instant comparison of local and Greenwich time, which converts to a longitude. The only catches are a slight parallax and that even a small error in the measurement leads to a much greater error in the actual location.

On Cook's trip, the duty of carrying out these measures fell to Charles Green, an astronomer. He was there mainly to observe the transit of Venus across the sun, as seen from Tahiti, but he also fixed many longitudes. On one occasion, as their ship drifted close to a reef, Green, Charles Clerke (the master's mate), and Mr Stephen

Forwood (the gunner), were 'engaged in taking a Lunar'. It is a measure of the calmness of Cook's crew that, as the ship moved closer to mortal peril, their first thought was to obtain the longitude, a process that Green recorded in his log like this:

> These observations were very good, the limbs of sun and moon very distinct, and a good horizon. We were about 100 yards from the reef, where we expected the ship to strike every minute, it being calm, no soundings, and the swell heaving us right on.

✝

COMPASSES

To get a bearing on the coast, sailors used a hand-held sighting compass, much like a prismatic compass. This let them steady the compass, peer through a sighting hole, and read off a bearing on the compass card, using a glass prism to see it. With practice, bearings could be read within a couple of degrees, and even more accurately on land, so long as the iron in the ship (or in the ground they were standing on) was not playing a role.

One complication, however, is that true north, the direction of the north geographical pole, is not usually the same as magnetic north, the direction in which the north-seeking pole of the compass points.

Worse, the difference changes with time and from place to place. It took time for people to work out what caused the variation, which relates mainly to the magnetic poles of the planet being different from the geographic poles (the south magnetic pole actually lies in the Southern Ocean, a long way from what we usually mean by 'the South Pole'). By Banks' time, this phenomenon was well understood, though some of the finer points like changes in Earth's magnetic field and other issues were still to be worked out. Here is Banks, just before he reached Botany Bay, describing a discussion with the master of the ship:

> The Variation is here very small, he says: he has three times crossd the line of no variation and that at all those times as well as at this he has observd the Needle to be very unsteady, moving very easily and scarce at all fixing: this he shewd me: he also told me that in several places he has been in the land had a very remarkable effect upon the variation, as in the place we were now in: at 1 or 2 Leagues distant from the shore the variation was 2 degrees less than at 8 Lgs distance.

A Kater's compass was essential. Thomas Mitchell mentions an Aboriginal youth trying to steal one from his pocket, Leichhardt carried one, so did Oxley and Grey. Charles Darwin noted in *The Voyage of the Beagle* that Mr Usborne had a small one that was stolen by birds in South America. Sir Thomas Brisbane, the most scientific governor of New South Wales, owned one, and in 1854 Darwin's cousin, Francis Galton, listed a Kater's compass as an essential item for 'travellers' (explorers), who should also own a sextant, two mountain barometers, two thermometers and a good pocket chronometer. Sir John Franklin took a Kater's compass when he ventured into polar waters in search of the North-West Passage.

Designed by Captain Henry Kater in 1811, the original Kater's compass used a mirror to allow the user to read a scale while simultaneously observing a distant object. In other words, it allowed you to take a bearing on a distant object in much the same way as a prismatic compass did. The prismatic compass was developed the following year and Kater's name was transferred to this improved version.

There is one further compass type to consider, and this appears, frustratingly, to be the most mysterious. Tucked in among David Carnegie's exhaustive 1896 packing list, there is a reference to '2 prismatic compasses, 2 steering compasses (Gregory's pattern)'. Sydney author Kieran Kelly tells me that the surveyor with the Jardine expedition to Cape York in 1864 was issued with a Gregory compass. (Kelly says this is hardly a surprise, given that Archibald Richardson, the surveyor, was employed by the government, so his boss was none other than Augustus Gregory, who had invented it!)

We can probably discount any untoward influence from Gregory, though. The Gregory compass was also greatly admired by Ernest Giles, who found it far easier to use than any other. He parted regretfully with one of them when he sent Gibson off to get help in what is now the Gibson Desert in 1874.

He then said if he had a compass he thought he could go better at night. I knew he didn't understand anything about compasses, as I had often tried to explain them to him. The one I had was a Gregory's Patent, of a totally different construction from ordinary instruments of the kind, and I was very loth to part with it, as it was the only one I had. However, he was so anxious for it that I gave it him, and he departed. I sent one final shout after him to stick to the tracks, to which he replied, 'All right,' and the mare carried him out of sight almost immediately. That was the last ever seen of Gibson.

In 1875, Giles would write of his travels: 'At seventy-eight miles from Ooldabinna, having come as near west as it is possible to steer in such a country on a camel—of course I had a Gregory's compass … ', but he was by no means finished praising the inventive Mr Gregory:

Augustus Gregory was in the West Australian field of discovery in 1846. He was a great mechanical, as well as a geographical, discoverer, for to him we are indebted for our modern horses' pack-saddles in lieu of the dreadful old English sumpter horse furniture that went by that name; he also invented a new kind of compass known as Gregory's Patent, unequalled for steering on horseback, and through dense scrubs where an ordinary compass would be almost useless, while steering on camels in dense scrubs, on a given bearing, without a Gregory would be next to impossible; it would be far easier indeed, if not absolutely necessary, to walk and lead them, which has to be done in almost all camel countries.

Kieran Kelly says the compass was never patented in Australia, and he speculated that it might have been recorded in some way in Britain. He later paid for a search of patent records in Britain, but found nothing. There is another possibility: the strictly correct pronunciation of 'patent', now little used, is *pattent*, not *paytent*. Possibly 'pattern' has been misunderstood as 'patent' at some stage.

Kelly explains the instrument as a saddle-mounted compass, strapped across the pommel, but says the instrument's exact nature is not known. The explorer's nephews left a 'Gregory pocket compass' to the Royal Geographical Society, Queensland, but it was stolen during World War II. Sadly, the Gregory compass was so simple, neat and obvious, that nobody bothered to write down exactly what it was all about. It must have been a clever bit of science, all the same.

In all sorts of ways, the compass was remarkably useful: given even a simple compass, and some way of measuring angles, you can do quite a lot. For example, the *Bounty* mutineers never expected William Bligh and his colleagues to survive when they pushed the loyalists off in a ship's boat with minimal food, water and navigational equipment. They did this as a less bloody way of committing murder, being sure that those in the boat were condemned to death. The boat's crew made it because Bligh knew the latitude of Timor, and sailed west till he found a bit of Australia, then north until he ran out of Australia, then west until he bumped into Timor.

It was all plane sailing, a method of treating the curved surface of the planet as a succession of flat surfaces. Today, people tend to spell it 'plain' sailing but, originally, it was a form of navigation on a plane that dodged the need for spherical trigonometry. On a sphere, the shortest distance between two points is a great circle, and if you fly the great circle, say, from Sydney to London, you will actually find yourself flying somewhat to the south at one point. If you get the bearing of London from Sydney and head off in that direction, you will go further than on the great circle route, or miss your target altogether. That makes the brain hurt, so simple sailors used plane sailing whenever they could.

RINGS, HOOKS, ASTROLABES AND KAMALS

Sailing north–south or east–west was always best because doing that only required a compass. In fact, you don't even need a compass to stay in the same latitude. A simple latitude hook—a stick with a viewing hole to look at a star on one end, and a marker to line up with the horizon—is enough. Hold this at arm's length, with the horizon marker on the watery horizon, see if the marker is above or below the hole, then adjust accordingly. Looking north, you will find the pole star, Polaris, as your reference point; in the south you need to imagine some lines in the sky, involving the Southern Cross and its pointers, lines that intersect at the South Celestial Pole, but it can be done. The people of the Pacific navigated quite happily with such simple instruments. Arabic traders used a slightly more sophisticated version of the same thing, a *kamal*.

On land, the altitude of the sun can be fairly accurately gauged with an astronomical ring, a simple suspended hollow cylinder with a small hole for the sun's light to shine through. This hangs vertically by gravity, and allows would-be explorers to note when the sun reaches its highest point in the sky, marking local noon.

Real navigation at sea began with the astrolabe, which was certainly known in England in 1391, when Geoffrey Chaucer wrote a *Treatise on the Astrolabe*, the first technical manual that we know about. Chaucer probably gathered and combined information from a number of foreign sources, but this marks the start of serious offshore navigation by the Europeans. The astrolabe was probably developed by the Greeks, and the name means 'star-taker', because it could gather a variety of information about any star. Where a latitude hook could only measure distance above the horizon, the astrolabe could also give you the azimuth, the bearing of a star away from true north.

As camel trains made their way across the dry country of north Africa and central Asia, astrolabes would have been used to keep them at the correct latitude to find towns or water, but there would have been a trade-off between large instruments with reduced error and small instruments offering greater portability. This same compromise forced itself on the explorers.

At sea, strong winds made a small astrolabe easier to use, and because it needed to hang by gravity on a rocking ship, they were typically heavy. Vasco da Gama got around the size issue by going ashore at key places with a large astrolabe. Columbus also had an astrolabe, but these were less than successful instruments. All the same, astrolabes had one advantage over some of the earlier instruments: they were aligned vertically by gravity and so needed no horizon. Every instrument needs a reference point and, in some ways, using gravity was the best solution.

These crude tools have built-in errors. The latitude hook is held at arm's length, but if you move your shoulder, the distance from eye to hand will change. The *kamal* had a knotted string that was clenched behind the front teeth, reducing the error, but all sightings involve a degree of guesswork—and hope.

BAROMETERS

Many explorers used barometers to measure altitude, though Allan Cunningham naïvely recorded a barometer altitude of '2984 feet', claiming rather more precision than would be wise. A variation of

1 inch, some 2.5 centimetres, equates to an altitude change of 1000 feet (305 metres). Under the best of laboratory conditions, the smallest measurable difference would be the equivalent of 30 feet (9 metres), so giving four significant figures is several steps too far. He noted that a nearby point was 'several feet higher', and so concluded that the Great Dividing Range above Port Macquarie is 'upwards of 3,000 ft. above the level of the sea', a safer approximation. Later, he reported an altitude determination of 3218 feet, again making an excessive claim for accuracy.

Eyre set out with two barometers, one of them provided by the governor, but within a few days reported that:

> Upon examining the barometers to-day, I was much concerned to find that they were both out of order and useless; the damp had softened the glue fastening the bags of leather which hold the quicksilver, and the leathers that were glued over the joints of the cisterns, and so much of the mercury had escaped, before I was aware of it, that I found all the previous observations valueless. I emptied the tubes and attempted to refill them, but in so doing I unfortunately broke one of them, and the other I could not get repaired in a satisfactory manner, not being able, after all my efforts, to get rid of some small air bubbles that would intrude, in spite of every care I could exercise.

This was a problem later, when Eyre went to name a mountain after a certain Mr Serle, as requested by the governor. While he could map the mountain and name it, he could not record its altitude, despite having to climb it anyway because of the triangulation imperative (the need to take bearings from every prominence).

If only he'd known there was another way! The temperature of boiling water falls in a predictable way at lower pressure, and pressure drops predictably with higher altitudes. The boiling point of water reflects the pressure and so indicates the altitude. In 1846, Charles Sturt calibrated a barometer and a thermometer, establishing that his thermometer read 212.25 degrees Fahrenheit (100 degrees Celsius) when water boiled at sea level. Later, he found the boiling point of water near Lake Torrens was 212.75 degrees Fahrenheit (100.4 degrees Celsius), measured at a point about 100 feet (30 metres) above the lakebed.

To Sturt, this meant the lake surface was well below sea level, but it could also have been a local 'high' passing over the area at the time. By 1881, when the Queensland government geologist, Professor Jack, went out to help survey a new railway line, this was better understood. The Transcontinental was planned to link the Gulf of Carpentaria to Brisbane, and on down to Bourke to link in Sydney and Melbourne, but the way needed mapping. Professor Jack wrote that he would need to recalculate his altitude estimates once he had sea-level readings for the matching days.

Barometers and thermometers were fragile. Sturt's thermometer broke the day after he took the Lake Torrens boiling point, and instruments made of glass and mercury were a challenge at the best of times. Sturt wrote in August 1844:

The box of instruments sent from England for the use of the expedition had been received, and opened in Adelaide. The most important of them were two sextants, three prismatic compasses, two false horizons, and a barometer. One of the sextants was a very good instrument, but the glasses of the other were not clear, and unfortunately the barometer was broken and useless, since it had the syphon tube, which could not be replaced in the colony. I exceedingly regretted this accident, for I had been particularly anxious to carry on a series of observations, to determine the level of the interior. I manufactured a barometer, for the tube of which I was indebted to Captain Frome, the Surveyor-General, and I took with me an excellent house barometer, together with two brewer's thermometers, for ascertaining the boiling point of water on Sykes' principle. The first of the barometers was unfortunately broken on the way up to Moorundi, so that I was a second time disappointed.

Cunningham lost a barometer when a horse carrying it fell, and complained that it was impossible to carry barometers and other delicately constructed mathematical instruments at that time, adding that he could still not find anybody in the colony able to repair the damage a year later.

Life was easier for instruments on board a boat or ship. Phillip Parker King was able to take both barometer and hygrometer readings throughout his voyages, and the *Beagle* carried both of these instruments as well.

Leichhardt may have carried some unusual items, like a brass-hilted sword, but he felt later that there were some deficiencies in his equipment.

> I had frequently reason to regret that I was not better furnished with instruments, particularly Barometers, or a boiling water apparatus, to ascertain the elevation of the country and ranges we had to travel over. The only instruments which I carried, were a Sextant and Artificial Horizon, a Chronometer, a hand Kater's Compass, a small Thermometer, and Arrowsmith's Map of the Continent of New Holland.

Arrowsmith's map, incidentally, was a key item. It is easy to get a measure of latitude from the sun or stars, and because Leichhardt had a reliable outline map of the coast, he was able to tell when it would be necessary to turn west to meet the base of the Gulf of Carpentaria. The map also showed the mouths of a number of rivers, allowing him to guess his longitude so long as he could match up the rivers.

In 1873, Giles climbed a mountain with 'all the apparatus necessary for so great an ascent: thermometer, barometer, compass, field glasses, quart pot, waterbag, and matches'. The water, he reported, 'boiled at 206 degrees, giving an elevation of 3085 feet above the level of the sea, it being about 1200 feet above the surrounding country'. On Mount Ferdinand, water boiled at 204 degrees, giving an altitude of 4131 feet—again, spurious accuracy was the order of the day.

In the large military establishment of Major Mitchell, one man was the designated barometer carrier, just as others were the blacksmith, the two carpenters, the shoemaker, the chainman and the butcher. There was some economy in Mitchell's party, as the butcher was also the shepherd, but the barometer carrier had just one function. On Kennedy's Cape York expedition, the mountain barometer was carried by botanist William Carron, one of the few to survive and tell his tale.

By the 1850s, one change was apparent. The aneroid barometer was invented in 1843 in France, and Augustus Gregory took one with him in 1855, apparently the first Australian explorer to do so. Now explorers had a small, robust and easy-to-carry instrument that anybody could use. Five years later, Wills left certain equipment behind at Cooper's Creek with Brahe, so that observations could be made:

> I have handed over to him for that purpose an aneroid barometer, Number 21,543, and four thermometers, two for dry and wet bulb observations, and the others for temperature of water, etc.

Nothing is ever indestructible, and in 1861 we find Francis Gregory describing repairs to 'the aneroid barometer, which had been crushed nearly flat by the fall of a horse; fortunately, however, without injury to the vacuum vase'. Twelve years later, Peter Warburton would record a catastrophe:

I now find my aneroid barometer is spoilt. This is a great misfortune, as I don't know when it got injured, and therefore cannot tell the date up to which its daily readings can be relied upon. I never anticipated such an instrument going wrong; but it was a great mistake on my part not to have taken a second one. I have three watches constantly going; and perhaps an explorer should have each instrument into triplicate, that he may more readily detect the one in error.

And that from somebody who attacked Herschel Babbage for carrying too much equipment! Perhaps Warburton had learned by then, after he had to send one of his party back some hundreds of miles to get some camel medicine he had failed to pack.

When it came to dumping things, instruments were among the last to go. Here Adoniah Vallack, one of the naval rescue party that came to save Edmund Kennedy's men from the coast of Queensland, describes the evacuation of William Carron, Edmund Kennedy's botanist:

We looked over the tent, asked Carron for what important things there were, and each laid hold of what appeared to be of most value, the captain taking two sextants, other parties fire-arms, &c., &c. 'Come along,' again and again Jackey called out, and the captain too, whilst they were half way down towards the creek, and Barrett and I loading ourselves. I took a case of seeds, some papers of Carron's, a double gun, and pistol, which, together with my own double gun and brace of pistols, thermometer, and my pockets full of powder and shot, was as much as I could manage.

✝

JETTISONING AND HIDING THINGS

Survival depended on knowing what to leave behind and when to leave it. Several explorers took boats into strange and apparently improbable places. Oxley was one of them, but he had no qualms about abandoning his boats along the Lachlan River when they no longer suited his needs. His instructions made it clear that he was to use the boats if possible to move his provisions and equipment, to avoid 'the tedious process of carrying them by land on the backs of horses, through a woody and intricate country'. That aside, he had a free hand.

As the boat option closed when he left the Lachlan in May 1817, Oxley abandoned the boats and moved on, as Allan Cunningham described it, 'leaving under the boats all weighty iron tools that we might reasonably conclude we should not require on our new course', and hoping that they would still be there at a later date. Then off they went, with George Evans, a tree-blazer and a perambulator driver at the front, finding, marking and measuring the way.

A month later, they were feeling the strain, so they 'overhauled the ironwork', and 'we left ten pairs of horse shoes, and some of the less useful parts of the boat builder's tools' on a tree. Later, Oxley may have regretted leaving the tools, as he had had problems re-crossing the Lachlan River, by now spilling over its banks. The next year, on the Macquarie River, the packhorses were strained to the limit, loaded with 350 pounds (159 kilograms) each after they 'relinquished every thing that was not indispensable', but they started out trying to fashion a carriage so they might haul a boat with them. In the end, they had to give up on the scheme, but Oxley's experience on a flooded Lachlan the previous year had clearly left an impression.

Just as Leichhardt was getting within sniff of Port Essington at the top of Australia and still deleting items, Charles Sturt was abandoning bacon and other heavy supplies in the middle of the continent. By then, Sturt was retreating from the parched desert of a drought-ridden central Australia in a desperate race to get past the dwindling waterholes and back to safety.

Most of the time, food was the one thing you did not leave behind. It was too hard to replace.

7.

Feeding the hungry explorer

THERE IS A WEIGHT LIMIT TO THE FOOD AN ADULT HUMAN CAN CARRY, and this sets a limit to how far you go unless you can live off the land, catching food as you go. Faced with limited choice, quite a few of the explorers' bush menu items sound more at home in the cauldron of Macbeth's witches than in the intestines of a human: camel foot, dingo pup, koala, snake, dead fish, crow, lowans' eyes, joey, bat, and even a crab taken from a dead shark's maw. All animal creation and most of the flora were fair game.

Christmas was a special time, and every explorer from George Evans to David Carnegie seemed to have a special Christmas experience—some pleasant, a few excruciating. On Christmas Day in 1813, Evans ate roast beef, while in 1821 Phillip Parker King and his crew shared a Yule feast of oysters, pudding and dumpling. In

1840, Eyre only took a slight break on Christmas Day, but in 1844 Leichhardt and his party had a Christmas dinner of suet pudding and stewed cockatoos.

Leichhardt's party made meals at other times of a 'sleeping lizard with a blunt tail and knobby scales', and he reports that when he sent a shot kangaroo back to the camp, it was greeted with delight 'as all they had for supper and breakfast, were a straw-coloured ibis, a duck, and a crow'. Six months from Port Essington, the party felt most bitterly the lack of flour and sugar, even though there was still some tea. When they killed two emus in July 1845, they feasted.

In 1855, Augustus Gregory killed a sheep for Christmas Day. Sturt and his men were bedevilled on the same day by flies and mosquitoes, and Burke and Wills' 1860 Christmas was marred by flies, mosquitoes and ants. On 23 December 1873, Giles and Gibson anticipated Christmas Day and dined two days early on pudding and rock wallaby. Further north, Peter Warburton wrote two days later that he would be thankful for the pickings of any pig's trough. 'Our last Christmas at Alice Springs was miserable enough, as we then thought, but the present one beats it out and out', he complained. In 1894, David Carnegie greeted a shower of rain as an excellent Christmas present. Two years later, he celebrated Christmas by attending a corroboree at Halls Creek.

By 1839, Stokes understood the likely fate of any hidden items, and he was more careful than to leave valuable stores in any place where local people could find them and carry them away.

Knowing how impossible it was to avoid being tracked by the natives, should they wish it, even upon the hardest ground, and that in the event of their doing so any buried stores would be forthwith discovered, and yet anxious to disencumber the party of any superfluous load, I directed one of the men to take the 8-pound canister of preserved meat and throw it into a thick cluster of reeds and palms, about thirty yards distant ...

The meat was still in its hiding place on their return, four days later, but explorers often did not care about the fate of what they left behind if unnecessary items had to be discarded.

George Evans' Christmas Day roast beef was something of a novelty in 1813, because it came in a 'tin case'. In 1820, the practice of sealing meat in tins, to keep it sweet and also to keep animals from attacking it, was more common. All the same, King named a small peak on the Kimberley coast after the maker of the tinned meat they ate there. It is still on the map, at 14°58'S, 125°30'E.

A steep peaked hill near our landing-place was named Donkin's Hill after the inventor of the preserved meats; upon a canister of which our party dined. This invention is now so generally known that its merits do not require to be recorded here; we had lately used a case that was preserved in 1814 which was equally good with some that had been packed up in 1818. This was the first time it had been employed upon our boat excursions and the result fully answered every expectation, as it prevented that excessive and distressing thirst from which, in all other previous expeditions, we had suffered very much.

Carnegie, at the end of the century, was harsher:

> Tinned meat is good, sometimes excellent; but when you find that a cunning storekeeper has palmed off all his minced mutton on you, you are apt to fancy tinned fare monotonous! Such was our case; and no matter what the label, the contents were always the same—though we tried to differentiate in imagination, as we used to call it venison, beef, veal, or salmon, for variety's sake! 'Well, old chap, what shall we have for tea—Calf's head? Grouse? Pheasant?' 'Hum! what about a little er—*minced mutton*—we've not had any for some time, I think.' In this way we added relish to our meal.

Explorers simply could not afford to be fussy eaters. They had no shops, no stores to visit, and had to eat whatever was on offer. Some of them became quite expert at catching dinner, but it took time and practice. In 1838, Stokes was trying to flush out kangaroos by lighting a fire, and almost incinerated the would-be shooters when the fire got out of hand. By November 1839, he could report a successful long-range shot, bringing down a kangaroo that was going at speed, but a few days later he added in a footnote that such challenging shots could be avoided by knowing that kangaroos bound away from a threat and then change direction to head uphill.

I had now become quite an adept in this kind of sport. My plan was to direct a man to walk along near the river, where they are generally found, whilst I kept considerably above him and a little in advance, so that all those that were started running up from the bank in the curved direction, habitual with all kangaroos, passed within shot.

✝

EXTREME FOOD

The explorers were not experienced hunter–gatherers, but some of them took to the lifestyle and ate everything that crossed their paths. Others ate the food carried by bullocks, horses and camels until the burden was all gone, and then ate the beasts that had carried it. They would stop for a few days, smoke and dry some of the meat, gorge on the rest in much the way that Eyre had disapprovingly seen Aborigines over-indulging, then move on. They sometimes salted meat: both Carron and Leichhardt reported finding and using salt deposits to preserve meat.

In June 1789, Tench's party augmented their salt pork with a crow they had shot. Half a century later, in August 1839, Stokes was chased by a crocodile, and in November he decided it was time to turn the tables. He shot a crocodile with ball, and knocked it out. His crew roped the animal and began hauling it to shore, but as it showed signs of reviving, Stokes tells us he gave it a charge of shot to the head as a sedative. Arriving at the shore, the men began hauling the crocodile up the slope, only to realize with some alarm that the crocodile was assisting in the progress. In the hurry, one man fell and rolled himself into a ball to get out of the way.

Stokes said that if the beast had been further from the water, he might have tried 'Waterton's experiment', referring to the yarn told by English traveller, naturalist and eccentric, Charles Waterton, claiming he had ridden a cayman in South America, noting in his *Wanderings in South America*, 'Should it be asked how I managed to keep my seat, I would answer, I hunted some years with Lord Darlington's fox-hounds.'

Waterton wanted his cayman as a zoological specimen; Stokes just wanted his crocodile dead, but it was 'not before he had received six balls in the head, that he consented to be killed'. Stokes could then describe the meat, as 'by no means bad, and has a white appearance like veal'.

Leichhardt was a committed bush-tucker person, declaring flying foxes to be 'most delicate eating', and praising as food 'iguanas, opossums and birds of all kinds'. He even ate 'blue-mountainers' (rainbow lorikeets), as King had done, throwing them in a pot with dried emu, cockatoos and an eaglehawk. Emu was among his favourites, and in the end nothing was wasted:

> Upon making our camp, we cut part of their meat into slices, and dried it on green hide ropes; the bones, heads, and necks

were stewed: formerly, we threw the heads, gizzards, and feet away, but necessity had taught us economy; and, upon trial, the feet of young emus was found to be as good and tender as cow-heel.

Two months away from the end of their journey, things were getting desperate. They had eaten a sort of soup made by boiling bullock skin, which they thought tasted better than dried bullock meat, and then came an extreme, even for his omnivorous crew. Leichhardt needed to discard his entire collection of botanical specimens, just two months from Port Essington, but the greenhide wrapping of the specimens still had a use.

We enjoyed most gratefully our two wallabies, which were stewed, and to which I had added some green hide to render the broth more substantial. This hide was almost five months old, and had served as a case to my botanical collection, which, unfortunately, I had been compelled to leave behind. It required, however, a little longer stewing than a fresh hide, and was rather tasteless.

The geological specimens collected by the dead John Gilbert and the duplicate zoological specimens were also discarded. They were about to kill a bullock, and needed to carry the 130 pounds (59 kilograms) of dried meat it would yield—and now had one less animal to carry things. When push comes to shove, food comes first.

In 1873, Colonel Peter Warburton took off for Roebourne, on the north-west coast, starting in central Australia. The party was defined by race (as was the custom) as 'four other white men, two Afghans and a black boy'—with seventeen camels. Warburton temporarily lost his vision, and permanently lost the use of one eye and, as we shall see, one of the Afghans needed to have a finger amputated as a result of a scorpion sting. It also appears one of the men lost his reason and never fully recovered—and from a comment Warburton made later, this would appear to have been his son, Richard. But while all the men survived, only one of the camels was among them at the last. Some were lost, but the rest were eaten. Warburton wrote on 23 November, six weeks from the end of their trip:

> We have but five camels left—one a weak sickly cow. We may get a few days' work out of her, after this long rest, and I do not wish to kill her, first because she has not meat enough on her old bones to find us ten days' food, and secondly if I can save any camels to take into the settled parts of Western Australia, I should like to take a cow. It would cripple us greatly to kill a bull, but it would keep us probably for three weeks. No doubt the camel killing will read badly, but the only alternative we have is to sit down and die, and they after us, for they could not get a drop of water without our help. Whether we kill or whether we don't kill, we are in a bad plight, and cannot help ourselves.

Three days later, they had to kill a camel, and Warburton wrote exultantly, 'Boiled kidneys and tongue for breakfast; we can scarcely believe it.' Soon the meat ran out, and a week later he wrote, 'A camel looks very large, but gives little meat compared with a bullock, and we have not a scrap of anything else, not even a pinch of salt.' On 7 December, they killed another camel by moonlight and, while being driven almost mad by ants, they cut up the meat and jerked it. On 12 December, Warburton listed the day's menu:

Got some cockatoos, and had some camel's foot. This latter is a delicacy, but troublesome to cook. I shall no doubt appear to dwell too much on eating, but it is difficult for starving men to keep their minds from thinking of what they once had, and now so urgently need.

The next day, some of the fitter members of the party were sent to fetch help, leaving one weakened camel behind. Warburton reported eating a shag (a cormorant) for breakfast as though it were a meal fit for a king, and he hoped the remaining camel would not die before they could kill it for food. On 19 December, they could wait no more, and so they killed the second-last camel. Two days later, it was almost ready to eat, and Warburton could look forward to eating camel's foot again.

A beautiful day. Meat drying nicely, but there is very little of it, and that very poor. No wonder, as the beast was quite worn out, and had been carrying a load from February to December without a rest. We are boiling down the hide, and hope for good food from it; the head, feet, and tail are the treasures.

Given that the party had been dining on kite, bulrush roots, crows, shags, small fish, cockatoos (and the birds were all eaten whole, he assures us), perhaps one can see that the foot of the camel might well be perceived of as a delicacy. If Leichhardt liked emu foot, why not?

In 1873, Ernest Giles discovered lowans' eggs—'lowan' is a disused Aboriginal name for the mallee fowl, and the thin-shelled eggs weigh up to 250 grams or half a pound. His account is worth quoting in full.

There are much easier feats to perform than the carrying of Lowans' eggs, and for the benefit of any readers who don't know what those eggs are like, I may mention that they are larger than a goose egg, and of a more delicious flavour than any other egg in the world. Their shell is beautifully pink tinted, and so terribly fragile that, if a person is not careful in lifting them, the fingers will crunch through the tinted shell in an instant. Therefore, carrying a dozen of such eggs is no easy matter. I took upon myself the responsibility of bringing our prize safe into camp, and I accomplished the task by packing them in grass, tied up in a handkerchief, and slung round my neck; a fine fardel hanging on my chest, immediately under my chin. A photograph of a person with such an appendage would scarcely lead to recognition. We used some of the eggs in our tea as a substitute for milk. A few of the eggs proved to possess some slight germs of vitality, the preliminary process being the formation of eyes. But explorers in the field are not such particular mortals as to stand upon such trifles; indeed, parboiled, youthful, Lowans' eyes are considered quite a delicacy in the camp.

The following year, Giles was in desperate straits in what is now the Gibson Desert.

I was very footsore, and could only go at a snail's pace. Just as I got clear of the bank of the creek, I heard a faint squeak, and looking about I saw, and immediately caught, a small dying wallaby, whose marsupial mother had evidently thrown it from her pouch. It only weighed about two ounces, and was scarcely furnished yet with fur. The instant I saw it, like an eagle I pounced upon it and ate it, living, raw, dying—fur, skin, bones, skull, and all. The delicious taste of that creature I shall never forget. I only wished I had its mother and father to serve in the same way.

A year later, Giles was dining on dingo pups and lowans' eggs again, not because he had to, but because he wished to. In mid-1861, Wills found one fish choking on another, and ate them both.

Survival, it seems, counted more than prissiness, though Kennedy's party took a while to accept the idea of eating horseflesh, according to William Carron.

> This morning we commenced to prepare our breakfast of horse-flesh. I confess we did not feel much appetite for the repast, and some would not eat it at all; but our scruples soon gave way beneath the pangs of hunger, and at supper every man of the party ate heartily of it, and afterwards each one claimed his share of the mess with great avidity.

Strzelecki was in Gippsland in 1840, making scientific collections, and then pushing into thick scrub, headed for Melbourne. He and his party were forced to abandon their horses and packs, and tried to get by on one biscuit and a slice of bacon per day. Ernest Favenc said they reached Western Port 'in a most wretched condition, having subsisted latterly on nothing but native bears'.

Anything would do for food when people were desperate enough, but a conservative approach sometimes saved lives. Not all the plants and animals could be eaten with safety, and a few of the more adventurous explorers paid for the risks they took.

✟

POISONS AND
PROBLEMS

Some of the early Europeans were too arrogant to look at how locals managed the food, but time brought wisdom. The risk-taking began when Joseph Banks and his party saw the remains of cycad seeds by the fireplaces of the Aborigines and tried them, with ill effects. Later, two of the *Endeavour*'s precious hogs died from eating the same seeds. Banks later discovered, after leaving Australia behind, that there were ways of removing the poison from the seeds, so that they could be eaten.

Few explorers, though, could have surpassed Ludwig Leichhardt, who seems to have tested or eaten anything and everything that came in reach. The *Pandanus* palm produced a fruit that gave him sore lips and a blistered tongue; and the first time he ate it, he was attacked by violent diarrhoea.

In September 1845, he wrote that the heaps of the fruits around Aboriginal camps suggested that it could be neutralized, but he had no idea how to do it. He said the fruit appeared either to have been soaked or roasted and broken, to obtain the kernels, which he thought were then pounded between stones and washed thoroughly. Four days later, he knew more:

The natives, at this season, seemed to live principally on the seeds of *Pandanus spiralis*, [R. Br.] and *Cycas*; but both evidently required much preparation to destroy their deleterious properties. At the deserted camp of the natives, which I visited yesterday, I saw half a cone of the *Pandanus* covered up in hot ashes, large vessels [koolimans] filled with water in which roasted seed-vessels were soaking; seed-vessels which had been soaked, were roasting on the coals, and large quantities of them broken on stones, and deprived of their seeds. This seems to show that, in preparing the fruit, when ripe, for use, it is first baked in hot ashes, then soaked in water to obtain the sweet substance contained between its fibres, after which it is put on the coals and roasted to render it brittle when it is broken to obtain the kernels.

Carron also watched closely. *Castanospermum* is the poisonous Queensland black bean. He managed to get locals to explain to him that they soaked the seeds for five days, sliced them and dried them in the sun, then pounded them, moistened them, and baked them on a flat stone. He reported that it was not very palatable.

In 1861, one of Stuart's men ran into problems when he tried some wild food. The party found a palm with neither seeds nor blossoms on it, and one man tried the leaf stalk, which he found sweet, but he soon became sick and vomited most of the evening. The next year, another of Stuart's adventurers also suffered from an injudicious selection of food:

Last night, a little after sundown, Mr. Waterhouse was seized with a violent pain in the stomach, which was followed by a severe sickness, and continued throughout the night; this morning he is a little better. I think it was caused by eating some boiled gum which had been obtained from the nut-tree Mr. Kekwick discovered last year. When boiled it very much resembles tapioca, and has much the same taste. I also ate some of it yesterday, which occasioned a severe pain in the stomach, but soon went off. Some of the others also felt a little affected by it, but none so bad as Mr. Waterhouse; on others it had no effect whatever, and they still continue to eat it. Mr. Waterhouse looks so ill that I think it desirable not to move the party to-day, and trust by to-morrow he will be quite well.

The next day, Waterhouse was indeed better, and the party was able to move on, but most humans approached potential food cautiously. The animals, on the other hand, commonly ate blithely on, and sometimes perished. This seemed to be a special problem with camels and, according to Ernest Giles, it resulted from a mix of ignorance on the part of those travelling with the camels and the camels' feeding habits.

With their long necks, camels can grab snacks as they pass through the country, a bite here and a bite there. A few of the plants were able to bite right back. The only solution was to dose the camels with an emetic and then look to see what was vomited up and try to avoid it in the future, but it was a losing battle. Giles commented:

The shepherds in this Colony, whose flocks are generally not larger than 500, are supposed to know every individual poison-plant on their beat, and to keep their sheep off it; but with us, it was all chance work, for we couldn't tie the camels up every night, and we could not control them in what they should eat.

Stuart and Wills both had horses poisoned by plants, but Peter Warburton lost camels mainly to other causes. One was poisoned; four ran away; three were left behind in the desert, unable to move; seven were killed for food; and two survivors were left on the DeGrey River.

Once the explorers knew what to eat, how to find it and how to prepare it, longer-distance travel became possible, because food caught is food that does not need to be carried. But before that could happen, many unusual meals were consumed, and quite a few people suffered in the trials. There was also one poison that was taken quite deliberately, a poison that caused many problems.

THE DEMON RUM

Alcohol is in fact a mild poison, but it was common on the packing lists of explorers, though generally not for drinking. Some was intended for preserving specimens, and some for rather more peculiar reasons.

At Swan Hill those great overloaders Burke and Landells discarded the lime juice that might have prevented scurvy in the men, but retained the rum that Landells insisted the camels needed to avoid scurvy. Some 350 kilometres further north, at Kinchega station, local shearers managed to get some of the rum. This caused a blazing row when Burke ordered that the rest of the rum be abandoned, and Landells walked off, followed by the surgeon, Dr Beckler, who felt the second-in-command had been badly treated. After that, it was the Burke and Wills expedition. In the 1890s, Carnegie had learned the bitter lesson of earlier parties. This note appears at the end of his long list of stores:

> The brandy was for medicinal purposes only. Even had we been able to afford the room I should not have carried more; for I am convinced that in the bush a man can keep his health better, and do more work, when he leaves liquor entirely alone.

In 1865, Duncan McIntyre was looking for traces of Leichhardt, and he was shown a tree marked 'L'. Ernest Giles argued later that this was a mark left either by Landsborough, or by Leichhardt on his earlier 1844 expedition. McIntyre hailed it as a trace of Leichhardt's later expedition, and Ferdinand von Mueller arranged the funding of an expedition called 'The Ladies' Leichhardt Search Expedition', which went out with sixteen camels and 60 horses.

It ended in disaster, said Giles, when a certain doctor, the second-in-command, caused the men to panic and plunder the medicinal brandy while McIntyre was away with the camels fetching water. This doctor was the man who later became infamous as a 'blackbirder', a collector of indentured labourers from the Pacific Islands. Giles mentioned that, but curiously omitted the doctor's name. He was Dr James Patrick Murray, originally of Melbourne, one of the least savoury in a generally less-than-savoury trade.

Giles said that as soon as McIntyre's back was turned, Murray threw in the towel. He told the other men they were abandoned to die of thirst, but if there was no water at least he knew in which packs the brandy was stowed, because the bags were marked. The horses were already suffering dreadfully but, ignoring them, the doctor took a knife and ripped the marked bags open and extracted the brandy. One man stood back, the rest got stuck in, and the packhorses wandered away to die, taking their packs with them. McIntyre returned with water to find his expedition ruined.

Brandy was often used in the nineteenth century as a preservative for animal specimens, but Giles seems to have taken methylated spirits for specimens on his trips, given a comment he made about a small adventure one night. It is worth noting that scorpions will approach a campfire, and then circle around it, possibly attracted by the light and repelled by the heat.

On the evening of the 5th of October a small snake and several very large scorpions came crawling about us as we sat round the fire; we managed to bottle the scorpions, but though we wounded the snake it escaped; I was very anxious to methylate him also, but it appeared he had other ideas, and I should not be at all surprised if a pressing interview with his undertaker was one of them.

Medical uses for brandy were common. After Gore, one of Stokes' officers, was injured by a discharging gun, the wounded man asked that his hand be washed in brandy and bandaged, then they proceeded as if nothing had happened. Eyre did not specify the purpose, but took only a small amount of brandy on his expeditions, suggesting its uses were mainly medicinal.

On the 14th, I landed the stores, to arrange and pack them ready for the journey. They consisted of forty pounds of flour, six pounds of biscuit, twelve pounds of rice, twenty pounds of beef, twenty pounds of pork, twelve pounds of sugar, one pound of tea, a Dutch cheese, five pounds of salt butter, a little salt, two bottles of brandy, and two tin saucepans for cooking; besides some tobacco and pipes for Wylie, who was a great smoker, and the canteens filled with treacle for him to eat with rice.

The problem was that alcohol, in any portable form, was concentrated, and drinking it made you thirsty. Land explorers were always concerned about water, and so were those at sea, as they needed to find places to land to refill the water kegs with clean, sweet water. Sometimes, land explorers had to forget about clean and sweet so long as there was water and it was wet and, at a pinch, even semi-dry mud would do. John McDouall Stuart would not have turned his nose up even at dry mud.

8.

Nor any
drop to drink

HORSES NEED MUCH MORE WATER THAN CAMELS, and carry less equipment, but even camels must drink sometimes—and camel-equipped humans still need water. Wherever there was water for stock or crops, and feed for stock, agriculture would follow, meaning water was always a matter of interest, but many of the explorers found themselves in dry country, desperately seeking water for themselves and for their transport animals.

Horses are seriously thirsty, as many Aborigines learned with dismay when explorers arrived at their soaks to water their animals. A working horse under hot conditions needs as much as 70 litres of water a day. Camels can make some of their water from their food, but even camels need a good long drink every now and then. Sheep and cattle taken as future food need water as well.

Australia is a dry continent, but it is wrong to imagine it as a desert of hot Saharan dunes under blue skies. There are parts of the inland with dunes, but most of central Australia is arid, not desert. There are plants and there is water to be had, if you know where to look, but those who hailed from England's green and pleasant land had no notion of that. It had to be learned.

WATER SIGNS

At least three men, David Carnegie, Peter Warburton and Ernest Giles, probably forced Aborigines to show them where water was to be found; many more relied on Aboriginal signs and tracks to find 'native wells'. But the better bushmen used the same natural indicators the Aborigines relied on. As early as 1801, James Grant and Francis Barrallier followed the sound of frogs to water, but by 1817 Oxley knew the scream of the white cockatoo as a water indicator and Eyre and Leichhardt also used white cockatoos to find water.

King and Leichhardt looked out for freshwater birds, and Stuart in central Australia took any birds at all as a likely sign of water. He regarded diamond birds as a certain sign, and so did Ernest Giles. Wills also knew this and, with Giles, mentioned the trees that indicated subterranean water on dry streambeds. Perhaps this was just an accepted thing, as Stuart made a casual reference to 'water-bushes' at one point in his journal. King, Wills and Giles all mention following Aboriginal tracks to water, and Giles also followed emu tracks to water.

Stokes was one of many who regarded the presence of 'native fires' as an indication of fresh water somewhere about. Giles said, 'you might safely declare that because there is water there are sure to be smokes, and because there are smokes there are sure to be fires and because there are fires there are sure to be natives ...' Giles also believed that when there were signs of tree roots being tapped for water, the chances of finding other water would be poor, although this did not always hold.

He noticed that a mountain given the name Churchman (a Gregory family name) by Augustus Gregory was shown as having been visited by several other explorers. He deduced that, while there was no record of water on the mountain, it must be there. This is dangerous logic of course, since each visitor after Gregory may have gone there on the same argument, reinforcing the fallacy. In fact Giles was correct, and he was able to get water at a 'native well'.

✝

FINDING WATER

In the very first line of his book, Carnegie told his readers he was travelling with Lord Percy Douglas. Carnegie was the fourth son of the Earl of Suffolk, so he *was*, in fact, a minor 'Somebody' within the narrow sense the British have of rank by birth—and overly keen to make sure his readers knew it.

In terms of personality and charm, he seems to have been exactly the sort of two-dimensional villain we all love to hate, yet he managed to survive in the desert for some considerable time, which we might find creditable. He was a cad and a bounder, but he was a competent desert survivor. Unfortunately, his survival techniques were far from creditable. On one occasion he fed salt beef to a captured Aboriginal man to make him thirsty, so he would lead them to water, and on another he captured an 'old and hideous gin' for the same purpose.

> Sorry as I was to be rude to a lady, I had to make her prisoner, but not without a deal of trouble. 'Dah, dah, dah!' she shouted, scratching, biting, spitting, and tearing me with her horrid long nails, and using, I feel sure, the worst language that her tongue could command. I had to carry this unsavoury object back to her camp, she clutching at every bush we passed, when her hands were not engaged in clawing and scratching me. After her anger had somewhat abated she pointed out a rock-hole from which they had got their water.

Aside from showing them this offering, a 'stinking pit' that yielded 12 gallons (55 litres), she refused to cooperate. Carnegie and his colleagues held her for two days, convinced that only by enforced help like this could they find water and survive. She, of course, was trying to conserve a valuable resource of her community, and after a second day of captivity, during which she remained, in his words, obdurate and useless, they let her go.

Carnegie was not completely unsympathetic to the plight of the Aboriginal people, but he called them a dying race and his words on their attitudes and probable future come across as ignorant and uninformed. Perhaps we should love all our fellow humans—but I reserve the right to maintain a B list.

Is this fair to Carnegie? Probably not, but prejudices like his led to the disastrous if well-meaning excesses of the 'stolen children' scandal, even into the 1960s. This saw children, especially those who appeared fair of skin, being taken from their families and put into soul-destroying institutions, where their cultural values were systematically wiped out, while they were being taught skills that would make them useful servants of their betters.

While Carnegie was too silly, or arrogant, to hide what he had done, you have to wonder how common it was to capture an Aborigine as Carnegie did, and force him or her to lead explorers to water. At one point, Ernest Giles wrote, 'I only wish I could catch a native, or a dozen, or a thousand; it would be better to die or conquer in a pitched battle for water, than be for ever fighting these direful scrubs and getting none.' Warburton also used this unsavoury method, and taken with Carnegie's admission of doing so on two occasions, that must make us suspect that it was a fairly common occurrence.

✟

BY BARREL, BAG AND CALABASH

The problem with water, especially when horses were used, was that it had to be carried. Horses are thirsty animals, and if a horse carried nothing but water in dry country, it could carry enough for two days—for itself. No equipment, no food, nothing.

On even ground, Eyre used a dray to haul 85 gallons (about 380 litres) of water, but after a mere 14 miles (22 kilometres), the going was too hard for the horses. Sturt had a tank mounted in a cart, but it sprang a leak and proved useless. He later used bullock skins to carry water in a dray.

In country where water was generally plentiful, Leichhardt used a calabash or gourd that had been given to Charley by some Aborigines. It held about 3 pints (just over 1.5 litres) of water. They also used a stewpot to carry water, but they were lucky to get through. On Kennedy's expedition, there were two water kegs, and each man carried a can holding 5 pints (nearly 3 litres). They also had canvas water bags, used on one occasion, filled with air, as floats to get a cart across a river.

The idea of the canvas water bag was that as it filled with water, the threads expanded and the water was held inside, soaking slowly out, so the breeze could evaporate small amounts of water and keep the water cool. The design is usually credited to Mitchell, who was supposed to have been inspired by the kangaroo-skin waterbags used by Aborigines.

Augustus Gregory used both kegs and waterbags, and Wills mentioned waterbags as well. In 1862, Stuart had problems with his waterbags, which lost half their contents in a single day, and in 1874, Ernest Giles found himself with some large, dry waterbags, as Gibson had gone off with the smaller ones. The large bags needed to be soaked in water to 'tighten' the canvas, so water would stay in the bag, and there was not enough. He had to carry a 15-pound (6.8-kilogram) keg with 20 pounds (9 kilograms) of water in it. Peter Warburton found that even kegs could dry out, writing plaintively, 'Casks will not hold, and I cannot go without them.'

Babbage set out to find water in the desert by science. He paid £22.10.0 for a boring apparatus and a portable pump (no shovel-dug wells for him), 8 pounds of filtering paper costing £1.6.6 (no muddy water either!), wash bowls, footbaths, tin pannikins, water tanks (150 gallons and 900 gallons) costing £28.0.0, stills (to get fresh water from salt lakes), pumps and fittings for £45.15.0. At least he came back alive!

FOUL WATER

In most cases, finding salt water was a disaster—unless you were Stuart, or Burke and Wills, seeking the north coast of Australia. For them, salt water meant they had reached the sea. But when Charles Sturt found a concentrated salt spring issuing into the Darling it was bad news indeed, because in drought time the salt spring tainted the whole river downstream. Watkin Tench was equally disappointed when he went out in search of a reported river.

> We went to the place described, and found this second Nile or Ganges to be nothing but a saltwater creek communicating with Botany Bay, on whose banks we passed a miserable night from want of a drop of water to quench our thirst, for as we believed that we were going to a river we thought it needless to march with full canteens.

Almost every explorer had a horror story to tell about water, and quality was clearly a high priority. The governor's instructions in June 1801 to Barrallier, Grant and Paterson called for a report on whether or not the water of the Hunter was 'sweet and good', though clearness was not always a desirable quality.

Wills noted, on Christmas Day 1860, that one body of water had a 'suspiciously transparent colour and a slight trace of brackishness', perhaps suggesting that he knew salty water tends to have less in the way of suspended clay minerals. He certainly saw a drawback of some sort with clear water, and just a few days earlier he had written of delaying 'to refill the water-bags' with the milky water, which all of us found to be a great treat again. It is certainly more pleasant to drink than the clear water, and at the same time more satisfying.'

Allan Cunningham revealed an interesting insight long before Pasteur and others developed the germ theory of disease when he noted, 'All the water we could procure, which we brought from distant corrupted holes, was very foul and muddy and filled with animalcules, to destroy which we boiled and strained the water.' In this case, Cunningham should have waited just a little longer: 'We had scarcely left our resting place when we found water in a small hidden hole, tolerably good at which we supplied our horses.'

John Oxley was no more impressed than Cunningham with the first water source, saying, 'The water was so extremely bad that, pressed as we were by thirst, we could scarcely even by twice boiling it render it drinkable.'

Cunningham had tasted his share of seriously bad water, and so was willing to rate as 'very acceptable' a pool of water that he described as 'a quantity of about 12 gallons of water that had been stagnant for some time, but had acquired a sub-putrid taste'. Eyre found one lot of water unusable: straining it twice through a handkerchief did nothing for it, and boiling only thickened it. The water 'was a deep red colour, from the soil, and was certainly an extraordinary and unpalatable mixture'. Another sample he characterized as 'with an effluvia very like Harrowgate water'. Topping that, Leichhardt wrote in January 1845:

When I returned to the camp, I found my companions busily engaged in straining the mud, which had remained in the water-hole after our horses and cattle had drunk and rolled in it. Messrs. Gilbert and Calvert had discovered a few quarts of water in the hollow stump of a tree; and Mr. Roper and Charley had driven the horses and cattle to another water-hole, about two miles off.

If there were to be a competition for the most horrifying account of water, Charles Sturt would need to be listed as a finalist with this comment from April 1845:

> Although we had ourselves been without water for two days, the mud in the creek was so thick that I could not swallow it, and was really astonished how Mr. Browne managed to drink a pint of it made into tea. It absolutely fell over the cup of the panakin like thick cream, and stuck to the horses' noses like pipe-clay.

The expedition horses, it seems, were not overly thrilled: 'They drank sparingly however, and took but little grass during the night,' he wrote. Six months later, Charles Sturt described how Stuart 'poked his fingers into the mud and moistened his lips with the water that filled the holes he had made, but that was all'. Those who merely complain of having to resort to brackish or saline water really cannot compete, because brackish water was still drinkable, at least as Stuart saw it in 1859, on Davenport Creek.

At five miles came upon a beautiful spring in the bed of the creek, for which I am truly thankful. I have named this The Spring of Hope. It is a little brackish, not from salt, but soda, and runs a good stream of water. I have lived upon far worse water than this: to me it is of the utmost importance, and keeps my retreat open. I can go from here to Adelaide at any time of the year, and in any sort of season.

At this point, Stuart was in the region of the mound springs which formed when artesian water bubbled up through the ground and slowly left behind deposits of salts that built up, raising the characteristic mounds. These leakage points on the edge of the Great Artesian Basin are there to this day, complete with attendant diamond birds, though less valuable than they were thanks to the amount of water that has been enthusiastically drawn out by bores driven into this supposedly inexhaustible supply, which turned out not to be quite as inexhaustible as people thought.

Wills, in early 1861, complained about water that had 'a disagreeable taste, from the decomposition of leaves and the presence of mineral matter, probably iron'. By 1862, Stuart was becoming more scientific: 'Last night I tried some citric acid in the water of the Finke, and it caused it to effervesce, showing that the water contained soda.'

Ernest Giles came late to the competition, but began well with references like 'our pool of slime'. That was just a warm-up, and in November 1873 he offered this description:

I found the hole was choked up with rotten leaves, dead animals, birds, and all imaginable sorts of filth. On poking a stick down into it, seething bubbles aerated through the putrid mass, and yet the natives had evidently been living upon this fluid for some time; some of the fires in their camp were yet alight. I had very great difficulty in reaching down to bale any of this fluid into my canvas bucket. My horse seemed anxious to drink, but one bucketful was all he could manage. There was not more than five or six buckets of water in this hole; it made me quite sick to get the bucketful for the horse.

The next day, Giles was still at the same source:

It was an exceedingly difficult operation to get water out of this abominable hole, as the bucket could not be dipped into it, nor could I reach the frightful fluid at all without hanging my head down, with my legs stretched across the mouth of it, while I baled the foetid mixture into the bucket with one of my boots, as I had no other utensil. What with the position I was in and the horrible odour which rose from the seething fluid, I was seized with violent retching. The horse gulped down the first half of the bucket with avidity, but after that he would only sip at it, and I was glad enough to find that the one bucketful I had baled out of the pit was sufficient. I don't think any consideration would have induced me to bale out another.

Giles was no weakling, and drank water that was 'yellowish, but pure'. David Carnegie took what was available as well, but his stoicism deprives him of a crown probably within his grasp. He said that he drank water so bad that the camels would not touch it, which still made 'excellent bread, and passable tea', noting that 'Man, recognising Necessity, is less fastidious than animals'. He certainly understood what had to be borne, and 'straining the putrid water brought by me through a flannel shirt, boiling it, adding ashes and Epsom salts, we concocted a serviceable beverage'.

Sometimes water was more available, but those were often the times when something nasty lurked beneath the surface, especially in northern Australia.

✝

LETHAL WATER

Stokes was at first ignorant that crocodiles, 'wholesale gastronomers', as he dubbed them, were in the area of Escape Point in February 1838, when he and two colleagues were trapped by the rising tide. By March, he knew all about them, and was surprised in August 1839 to see how Aborigines swam across what he took to be crocodile-infested waters. This may explain why, in October of that year, Stokes was willing to swim a creek himself.

I had stripped to swim across a creek, and with gun in hand was stealthily crawling to the outer edge of the flat where my intended victims were, when an alligator rose close by, bringing his unpleasant countenance much nearer than was agreeable. My gun was charged with shot, and the primitive state of nudity to which I had just reduced myself, precluded the possibility of my having a second load. To fire therefore was useless, and to retreat difficult, for I had wandered from the boat some distance across the bank, on which the water was fast rising. Thought, there was no time for, and before my companions could have reached me, the tide would have flooded the place sufficiently to enable the alligator to attack me at a disadvantage. My only chance of escaping the monster was to hasten back to the boat, and to cross the last creek before the alligator, who appeared fully aware of my intentions.

It was now, therefore, a mere matter of speed between us, and the race began. I started off with the utmost rapidity, the alligator keeping pace with me in the water. After a sharp and anxious race, I reached the last creek, which was now much swollen; while the difficulty of crossing was aggravated by my desire to save my gun. Plunging in I reached the opposite shore just in time to see the huge jaws of the alligator extended close above the spot where I had quitted the water. My deliverance was providential, and I could not refrain from shuddering as I sat gaining breath upon the bank after my escape, and watching the disappointed alligator lurking about as if still in hopes of making his supper upon me. Waiting till the monster came close, I took a deliberate aim at his eye, which had only the effect of frightening him a little.

The crocodiles, 'alligators' to most of the explorers, inspired an instinctive fear. We can see this in the first report of an alligator, in the journal of Arthur Bowes Smyth, written in Sydney in February 1788: 'An alligator, ab't 8 feet long, was seen close by where I go to birdlime just behind the camp, and has been seen among the tents at night more than once.' Sydney is far to the south of crocodile territory, so this was presumably a rather smaller goanna, a monitor lizard.

By 1818, Allan Cunningham was reporting alligators 6 and 7 feet (1.8 and 2.1 metres) long, 'whose terrific ghastly heads appeared occasionally on the surface of the water'. On the same day, King noted in his journal that alligators were seen resting on the mud, making them unwilling to stay up the river overnight. He promptly dubbed the river they were on the Alligator River.

The crocodiles they saw there must have been impressive, because in August 1819, King wrote, 'As we returned several alligators swam past the boat; but they were neither so large nor so numerous as those of the Alligator Rivers; the largest not being more than twelve or thirteen feet long', though he noted in 1821 that he had never seen one more than 20 feet (6 metres) long. At times, alligators could even be the cause for hope, of a sort, as King noted in September 1819.

In the evening [since we had lately seen no appearance of sharks] the people were allowed to bathe; but they had no sooner finished, and everyone on board, than an alligator swam past the vessel. The appearance of this animal revived some hopes of our yet finding fresh water and also that the gulf would terminate in a river; the breadth here is about a mile and a half and the rise of the tide about twenty-one feet: the ebb set at the rate of three knots per hour and the water was very muddy; but at low tide, upon being tasted, it still retained its saltness.

In fact, some of King's crew seem to have become quite used to the crocodiles, though clearly not understanding that the estuarine crocodile is as equally at home in salt as in fresh water. They camped by a river (in itself fairly risky, as we would see it now), but to stop the timbers of the boat drying and shrinking, the boat was left in the water.

... as it was prudent, if possible, to keep the boat afloat, one of the men was stationed in her for that purpose; but, overpowered by fatigue, he fell asleep and the boat in a short time was left dry upon the mud; the party on shore were continually disturbed during the night by what was thought to be the rushing of alligators into the water beneath them, but the noise was probably occasioned by stones and lumps of mud falling into it as the tide ebbed; a splash, however, that they heard on the opposite side was very likely an alligator, for they had seen one swimming as they pulled up the river. On hearing this Mr. Roe became very much alarmed on account of the boat-keeper, but no pains to apprize him of his danger had any effect: the only reply that could be got from him was, 'Damn the alligators,' and the next moment he was asleep again; fortunately for him no alligator came near enough to make him repent his foolhardy insensibility.

Leichhardt had no idea the Gulf of Carpentaria harboured any crocodiles until his party saw one in June 1845. Wherever explorers looked, dangers seemed to be lurking. Death and disfigurement were just around the corner; starvation, death by parching, disease, flood and wildfire all threatened, and then there were the largely imagined fears of attack by the 'savages'.

✝

9 ·

Aboriginal relations

IN SPITE OF FREQUENT WHITE MISBEHAVIOUR, there were many Aborigines who assisted in the explorers' 'discoveries'. Some of these were companions who spoke a little English; others were just people who met the explorers in the bush, or on the shores, and chose to be friendly and helpful, using sign language, gestures and sand maps. In most cases, the first encounters must have been a culture shock on both sides, though the Europeans had some notion at least that they would meet with 'Indians'. The Europeans needed to go gently, as one of Cook's party did, in 1770.

I sent some people in the Country to gather greens, one of which stragled from the rest, and met with 4 of the Natives by a fire, on which they were broiling a Fowl, and the hind leg of one of the Animals before spoke of. He had the presence of mind not to run from them [being unarm'd], least they should pursue him, but went and set down by them; and after he had set a little while, and they had felt his hands and other parts of his body, they suffer'd him to go away without offering the least insult, and perceiving that he did not go right for the Ship they directed him which way to go.

What the Aboriginal people made of these strange creatures would have depended on a number of things. Those who had heard of strangers might have heard bad things: the usual aggressive reactions of locals on the northern coast to naval exploration were probably related more to experience with trepangers (who visited regularly from Indonesia to collect bêche-de-mer). Any aggression or misunderstanding from either side would have set the scene for the future.

Cook's unnamed crewman who fell in with the Aborigines had the advantage that the pale strangers had been seen and assessed, so his gentle and unthreatening entry into their temporary camp was accepted as a harmless visit. As early as January 1788, First Fleeters were expressing a fear of the local inhabitants, as in this tale from Arthur Bowes Smyth at Botany Bay.

Their Huts or Wigwams are dispersed about and cat paths leading from one to the other and having wandered some distance into the woods in search of Insects & other natural Curiosities, I lost myself and could not find my way back to the

Wooding Party, which threw me into no small panic least I should meet with any of the Natives before I could extricate myself from the Labarynth I had got into ... but, I crawl'd along gently & had the good Luck to escape being noticed by them; & to my inexpressable Joy I shortly after got sight of the Bay.

✠

SPEARS, GUNS AND FRIENDSHIP

In February 1790, two years after the first flag was raised at Sydney Cove, Governor Arthur Phillip was of the opinion that where convicts had been wounded or killed, it was their own fault—that they had provoked the situations that led to them being hurt. After a misunderstanding in September 1790, Phillip was speared in the shoulder at Manly, but he ordered his men not to retaliate. Thanks to treatment by Surgeon John Harris, Phillip survived. (In 1818, William Blake was speared as Oxley's party moved down the coast to Port Stephens. They expected him to die, but Harris came to the rescue again and saved Blake's life.)

When John McEntire became the eighteenth convict speared to death in December 1790, Phillip's patience came to an end. An armed party was told to capture six men, two of whom were to be hanged, while the others were to be reprieved at the last minute. The original order was to catch and kill ten men and bring back their heads, but this watering-down mattered little, as a drummer boy and 52 men thrashed around in heat and sand, maddened by flies and mosquitoes, but caught nobody.

Some people suspected this was all Phillip had intended, that it was a matter of show, but feelings settled and most expeditions thereafter seem to have included Aboriginal helpers. By April 1791, some of the whites were even beginning to develop some cultural insights, as this tale from Watkin Tench reveals.

How easily people, unused to speak the same language, mistake each other, everyone knows. We had lived almost three years at Port Jackson [for more than half of which period natives had resided with us] before we knew that the word 'beeal', signified 'no', and not 'good', in which latter sense we had always used it without suspecting that we were wrong; and even without being corrected by those with whom we talked daily. The cause of our error was this. The epithet 'weeree', signifying 'bad', we knew; and as the use of this word and its opposite afford the most simple form of denoting consent or disapprobation to uninstructed Indians, in order to find out their word for 'good', when Arabanoo was first brought among us, we used jokingly to say that any thing, which he liked was 'weeree', in order to provoke him to tell us that it was good. When we said 'weeree', he answered 'beeal', which we translated and adopted for 'good'; whereas he meant no more than simply to deny our inference, and say 'no'—it is not bad.

John Macgillivray, who sailed on HMS *Rattlesnake*, was an enthusiast for gathering word lists, and he discovered the pitfalls of this habit while trying to get the word used for 'shin-bone' by the residents of Cape York. At various times and by different individuals, he was told names that he later discovered meant the leg, the shin-bone, the skin, and bone in general.

Some explorers like Hume, Sturt and Eyre had good relations with the Aboriginal people; some remained aloof and suspicious, like Stuart; some were positively inimical to the local inhabitants and their rights, like Hoddle, Mitchell and Carnegie. Let's start with the good news and work our way through to the villains.

The explorers started out under something of a disadvantage, because they mostly had little understanding and no appreciation of the Aboriginal culture. Even those exposed to Aborigines mostly saw only marginalized fringe dwellers in an expanding European society. Aboriginal cultural assumptions were generally dismissed as just the heathen beliefs of a bunch of savages, and any act of aggression to defend their rights was denounced as unwarranted.

However, not everybody shared this view: in 1840, Eyre discussed a case where a white boy had been speared, and commented:

> First, That our being in their country at all is, so far as their ideas of right and wrong are concerned, altogether an act of intrusion and aggression.
>
> Secondly, That for a very long time they cannot comprehend our motives for coming amongst them, or

our object in remaining, and may very naturally imagine that it can only be for the purpose of dispossessing them.

Thirdly, That our presence and settlement, in any particular locality, do, in point of fact, actually dispossess the aboriginal inhabitants.

Fourthly, That the localities selected by Europeans, as best adapted for the purposes of cultivation, or of grazing, are those that would usually be equally valued above others, by the natives themselves, as places of resort, or districts in which they could most easily procure their food. This would especially be the case in those parts of the country where water was scarce, as the European always locates himself close to this grand necessary of life. The injustice, therefore, of the white man's intrusion upon the territory of the aboriginal inhabitant, is aggravated greatly by his always occupying the best and most valuable portion of it.

Fifthly, That as we ourselves have laws, customs, or prejudices, to which we attach considerable importance, and the infringement of which we consider either criminal or offensive, so have the natives theirs, equally, perhaps, dear to them, but which, from our ignorance or heedlessness, we may be continually violating, and can we wonder that they should sometimes exact the penalty of infraction? do not we do the same? or is ignorance a more valid excuse for civilized man than the savage?

There is much more in the same vein, and Eyre reminded his readers that the brother of the speared boy had fired at some Aborigines just before the spearing, but those comments are enough to show that not all the explorers were unsympathetic to the Aborigines and their future. It has to be said, though, that even the sympathizers saw as the best of all possible worlds one in which Aborigines were drawn into the white man's culture, with the loss of their own. This, after all, was how the English treated other savages like the Irish, Welsh and Scots, and it had worked there, hadn't it?

John Macgillivray, for all that he dismissed their views as superstition, at least respected Aboriginal beliefs. After describing a dugong fishery in the Brisbane River, he wrote:

> The other is an undescribed porpoise, a specimen of which, however, I did not procure, as the natives believed the most direful consequences would ensue from the destruction of one; and I considered the advantages resulting to science from the addition of a new species of *Phocoena*, would not have justified me in outraging their strongly expressed superstitious feelings on the subject.

Few were harsher than Mitchell in his comments about the first Australians, but even he felt the need to admit that they had a few advantages. Here, for example, he begins with a strong attack on the Aborigines, but then admits that the savages at least have better teeth.

Their occupation during the day was only wallowing in a muddy hole, in no respect cleaner than swine. They have no idea of any necessity for washing themselves between their birth and the grave, while groping in mud for worms, with hands that have always an unpleasant fishy taint that clings strangely to whatever they touch ... If the naturalist looks a savage in the mouth, he finds ivory teeth, a clean tongue, and sweet breath; but in the mouth of a white specimen of similar, or indeed less, age, it is ten to one but he would discover only impurity and decay, however clean the shoes and stockings worn, or however fine the flour of which his or her food had consisted.

✝

T R A D E R S   A N D   T H I E V E S

There is a long and sad history of Aboriginal remains and artefacts being stolen. In 1817, Allan Cunningham records the removal of a cranium from a grave, saying that it would be taken away for further study, while his companion, John Oxley, wrote in his journal that all materials were returned to the grave after they had been examined. One of them, clearly, is telling an untruth. The following year, Cunningham described taking some Aboriginal remains to Lieutenant King, which King dismissed as being too imperfect to be worth preserving or carrying away.

Some three weeks earlier, King sent midshipman Bedwell to capture any local canoes as a reprisal for locals seizing some tools left onshore. That night, some of the locals apparently swam out to the boat to recover their property, and failing to do so, cut the painter of the whale boat and set it adrift. To Cunningham, these were mischievous natives, not the clever and resourceful warriors we might be inclined to see today. King, of course, was expected to bring back curios that would find their way to the learned men in England, and any sort of attack or affray was enough to justify seizing whatever could be found. On Australia's north coast, after one such incident, he wrote of the finds, which included a tool made from hoop-iron, material that he thought he must have left at Careening Bay the previous year. Other finds were more exotic:

> ... on searching about the grass we soon found and secured all their riches, consisting of water-baskets, tomahawks, spears, throwing-sticks, fire-sticks, fishing-lines, and thirty-six spears; some of the latter were of large size, and very roughly made, and one was headed with a piece of stone curiously pointed and worked.

Eyre, on the other hand, did not hold with wholesale theft, but he tried to trade from time to time, and even when he was faced with extremity, he tried to make a payment of some sort. On one occasion, he approached an Aboriginal camp, causing the inhabitants to flee and leave behind two small children. He looked around, took some muddy water from a kangaroo skin, and tied a red pocket handkerchief around one of the children by way of payment.

Leichhardt also believed in payment when he visited an encampment that had just been vacated.

> As I was in the greatest want of cordage, I took two of these nets; and left, in return, a fine brass hilted sword, the hilt of which was well polished, four fishing-hooks, and a silk handkerchief; with which, I felt convinced, they would be as well pleased, as I was with the cordage of their nets.

The following year, Leichhardt needed water containers and took two calabashes from a camp, leaving behind 'a bright penny'. He walked away, leaving many other Aboriginal possessions, including an iron tomahawk that showed, he said, that they were in contact with the coast.

Stuart recorded collecting some skeletal remains belonging to a child, saying only that he planned to take them back to Adelaide if they were still there on his return, but he seems to have made no other mention of these. Ernest Giles collected some nice curios while in the outback, but seems merely to have taken them, and David Carnegie saw no problems with just helping himself either.

> Quaintest of all these articles were the native 'portmanteaus,' that is to say, bundles of treasures rolled up in bark, wound round and round with string—string made from human hair

or from that of dingoes and opossums. In these 'portmanteaus' are found carved sticks, pieces of quartz, red ochre, feathers, and a number of odds and ends. Of several that were in this camp I took two—my curiosity and desire to further knowledge of human beings, so unknown and so interesting, overcame my honesty, and since the owners had retired so rudely I could not barter with them. Without doubt the meat-tins and odds and ends that we left behind us have more than repaid them. One of these portmanteaus may be seen in the British Museum, the other I have still, unopened.

His honesty, it seems, was forever being overcome. At one point, Carnegie made reference to 'a pearl oyster-shell, which was worn by the buck as a sporran' and which he later mentioned coyly was 'in my possession'. There is no mention of trading, but Carnegie noted that the party had a number of iron items, which we learn a little later had somehow become attached to the increasingly larcenous Englishman, who handed them over to Mr Panton, a police magistrate whom he classed as an expert. Rather than throwing the thief in the slammer, the magistrate declared excitedly that the iron tent peg came from the Leichhardt expedition. It would by then have been almost 50 years old, making this improbable, but Carnegie was not finished in his depredations. Shortly after, one of his party took an iron tomahawk, made from half a horseshoe, from its owner, but when it was illustrated in his book, the caption says rather less honestly: 'found about lat. 21 degrees 50 minutes, long. 126 degrees 30 minutes'.

Most of the other instances of aggression by Aborigines seem to be straightforward territorial defences, with the possible exception of the incident in which John Gilbert died, and this appears to have been provoked. Leichhardt and his party had been out in the field for fourteen months and were within two months of reaching Port Essington when they came under attack. John Roper and James Calvert were wounded and John Gilbert killed when Aboriginal warriors attacked the party at night.

According to John Macgillivray, this attack was provoked by the actions of Charley and Brown. Here is his explanation of events (it would be reasonable to assume that what Macgillivray called a 'gross outrage' was an act of rape).

Long afterwards the undoubted cause of this apparently unaccountable attack transpired in the acknowledgment, while intoxicated, by one of the persons concerned, that a gross outrage had been committed upon an aboriginal woman a day or two previously, by the two blacks belonging to the expedition.

10.

Injury and death

THE REAL WONDER IS NOT THAT SOME EXPLORERS DIED in the field, but that so few of them died there. Far too many went out unprepared for the country they walked or rode into, unready to deal with a sovereign people, unequipped to make repairs, and unaware of the basics of getting food and water in a strange country. They seem to have had a more fatalistic approach to life, and sometimes their conversations and thoughts sound to us just like the old Icelandic sagas, where Dark Events were always foreshadowed and underlined.

A few days before Gibson disappeared and died, he and Ernest Giles had a rather gloomy (and very saga-ish) discussion on death and exploration. Giles mentioned that it was the anniversary of the return of Burke and Wills to the DIG tree. This was their depot, where a support party should have been waiting for their return. As Gibson knew little of the story, Giles added more detail, mentioning that Wills' brother had died with Arctic explorer Sir John Franklin, seeking the North-West Passage. Gibson then volunteered that he lost a brother on that expedition as well, as Giles recorded:

> He seemed in a very jocular vein this morning, which was not often the case, for he was usually rather sulky, sometimes for days together, and he said, 'How is it, that in all these exploring expeditions a lot of people go and die?' I said, 'I don't know, Gibson, how it is, but there are many dangers in exploring, besides accidents and attacks from the natives, that may at any time cause the death of some of the people engaged in it; but I believe want of judgment, or knowledge, or courage in individuals, often brought about their deaths. Death, however, is a thing that must occur to every one sooner or later.' To this he replied, 'Well, I shouldn't like to die in this part of the country, anyhow.'

Giles was right, of course. There were many ways to die, and perhaps the most curious among them is the unknown danger that wiped out Leichhardt. This explorer ought to have learned from his earlier experiences, which included Aboriginal attack and the threat of death from thirst and starvation. Giles was one of the few to offer a sensible theory about Leichhardt's second expedition.

Leichhardt's first expedition had been on a shoestring budget, but after his triumphal reappearance in 1846, he had strong public support for his attempt to cross the continent. He travelled overland first from the Hunter River to the Darling Downs, leaving from there on 10 December 1846 with seven Europeans and two Aborigines. The expedition's stock included 270 goats, 180 sheep, 40 bullocks, fifteen horses and thirteen mules. This, with their flour, tea, sugar, and other usefuls, was to last them on a two year journey.

They took no medicines, got tangled in brigalow scrub, and were rained upon as they only had two ineffective calico tents. First they lost their sheep and goats, then the cattle and most of the horses and mules before turning up at a station on the Condamine on 6 July 1847. They had been out almost seven months and had found nothing new.

When they set out again in 1848, there were eight in the party including two Aborigines, 50 bullocks, thirteen mules, twelve horses, 270 goats and no sheep. Expecting to be out for up to two years, they had an inadequate 800 pounds of flour, 120 pounds of tea, 250 pounds of shot, 40 pounds of gunpowder and some sugar and salt. It seems Leichhardt planned to live off the land again, perhaps not a wise move for a march across central Australia.

Leichhardt had little knowledge of bushcraft and would have been a liability if he became trapped in dry country. That may have been what happened, but bushmen have wondered ever since why no traces of the explorer were found. Some of the iron implements, some of the iron frames made for the pack bullocks, ought to be out there, somewhere.

Writing in 1889, Giles accounted for the complete lack of any relics. The weather of northern Australia is part of the monsoon system that influences South-East Asia, with tropical cyclones pushing in during the Wet, mainly January and February, but often extending later.

Most of these storm systems sputter out over land, not far from the coast, but some push further in, delivering massive rainfalls into the catchments of the rivers that feed down into Lake Eyre. Giles knew this and, to him, it was the answer.

The Cooper is known in times of flood to reach a width of between forty and fifty miles, the whole valley being inundated. Floods may surround a traveller while not a drop of local rain may fall, and had the members of this expedition perished in any other way, some remains of iron pack-saddle frames, horns, bones, skulls, firearms, and other articles must have been found by the native inhabitants who occupied the region, and would long ago have been pointed out by the aborigines to the next comers who invaded their territories. The length of time that animals' bones might remain intact in the open air in Australia is exemplified by the fact that in 1870, John Forrest found the skull of a horse in one of Eyre's camps on the cliffs of the south coast thirty years after it was left there by Eyre. Forrest carried the skull to Adelaide.

✝

THE RIDDLE OF
BAXTER'S BONES

John Baxter, occasionally referred to as James Baxter, is a bit of a shadowy figure. He appears to have been with Eyre from almost his earliest days in the colonies, and he is often identified only as 'the overseer' in Eyre's accounts. Baxter was shot by one or the other of Joey and Yarry (though they may also have been Cootachah and Neramberein, as several authors use these names, though they do so without any real explanation of their source). These two New South Wales Aborigines, along with Wylie, who came from the Albany area, were travelling with Eyre and Baxter.

By all the evidence, Eyre was one of the most gentle and courteous men with Aborigines, yet his was the only party where one of the white members was killed by one of the Aboriginal members of the party. It was hard for Englishmen who had first crossed the world and then gone into the wilderness to understand that places were not the same in another culture. Some of them found it equally hard to accept that what they saw as crude tools, no more than a few stones and sticks, might be of value to the local inhabitants. Eyre was not one of those, and Baxter had been with him so long that he must have shared his employer's enlightened attitudes, yet Baxter died.

Eyre had attempted to travel north, been blocked by what appeared to be a single impassable salt lake with marshes (his 'horseshoe lake', which we will come to later), and headed west, along the Great Australian Bight. After several probing treks along the coast, he decided to try to force a way through to what is now Albany in Western Australia.

When they set out, the party had nine horses, a Timor pony with a young foal, six sheep, and some food. Eyre had set up caches of food in his earlier probes along the coast, and believed that he could crash through. It might have been easier if there had been sandhills all the way along, because by now Eyre knew how to dig for water at the base of sand dunes near the sea. But as he knew well from maps drawn by Flinders and others, this was not the nature of the coast. Much of it was high limestone cliffs offering no promise of easy water.

Eyre's party pushed off on 25 February 1841, and by 29 April 1841 they were into a seven-day period with no water as they walked along the second line of cliffs. The horses were suffering terribly, and while Eyre would have known from the maps that the cliffs would eventually end, giving way to water-bearing dunes, Joey and Yarry must have been alarmed. They were getting further from their homes (Wylie, at least, knew he was getting closer to home), and there was no water apart from the small amount they were carrying.

They had already experienced one period of thirst, from which they needed to recover for several weeks, at a place now called Eyre's Sand Patch. Eyre viewed the route ahead and saw the cliffs stretching out to the south-west: 'I at once knew, that when we left our present position, we could hope for no water for at least 140 or 150 miles beyond,' he wrote later.

A week before Baxter was killed, Wylie and one of the others headed off on their own, but after four days they returned. They could find no food, and were allowed to rejoin the party. So by 27 April, the Aboriginal members of the party thought the way ahead was impassable, but they knew where water could be found at Eyre's Sand Patch. They also knew there were supplies cached at Fowler's Bay, further back.

Whatever their motivation, Joey and Yarry wanted to head back to the east, and either decided to kill the sleeping Baxter while Eyre kept watch on the horses at some small distance, or Baxter awoke and realized they were stealing items to take with them. One way or another, Baxter was shot and fatally wounded. Eyre heard the shot, but when he got back to the camp he found Baxter dying and Joey and Yarry gone. They had taken all the serviceable firearms, all the visible ammunition, and much of the food and water.

Eyre was unable to dig a grave for Baxter, so he and Wylie wrapped the body in a blanket and left it on the surface before pushing west, full of fear. Somewhere in the bush, there were two desperate men who might stop at nothing to obtain the rest of the provisions—men who were armed with double-barrelled guns, while Eyre had two pistols and a rifle. According to Hamilton Hume, this rifle had a ball stuck in the breech after Baxter had tried to wash it when it was loaded, but Eyre mentioned using it later, in early May, so he had obviously managed to fix it by then.

On the first day, Joey and Yarry called from the bushes for Wylie to join them and threatened Eyre with the firearms, but Wylie stayed with Eyre, and as they pushed west with the horses, the two runaways gave up. Eyre later believed that the two had almost certainly survived, but they disappear from our story. Eyre and Wylie pushed on, finding richer vegetation and 'many recent traces of natives', all apparently heading to the west. On 3 May, they followed a steep 'native road' down to a point where they could dig for water at the base of the dunes, and eventually made it to Albany.

Baxter's body remained where it was, in an isolated spot, for many years. In 1878, William Graham was the telegraph stationmaster at Eyre's Sand Patch, and he organized a search party under the command of a telegraph line inspector called John Healy, who found parts of a saddle and human bones, but no skull.

The bones were scatted over 50 to 60 yards (45 to 55 metres), which is not uncommon when scavengers feed off any dead animal. A number of the bones were collected, along with the flintlock of a gun, perhaps the one that killed Baxter, and after being sewn into calico parcels by Mrs Graham, the relics were sent to Perth in the care of a police lance-corporal who was making a coastal patrol.

When they arrived in Perth, the bones and the flintlock seem to have been separated, and by 1927 the bones were missing. A Perth public servant tried to trace them between then and 1941, without success, and whether they went onto a rubbish dump or remain in three hand-sewn calico parcels labelled A, B and C in a cupboard in a cellar, the remains of Baxter are lost to our view.

✛

MEDICINES AND MEDICAL MEN

Baxter could not have been saved, but most explorers carried at least a few ointments, pills and potions. In the days before modern medicine, these were little better than snake oil: good perhaps to smear on a wound, but with limited effect. Most treatments were poisonous, evil-smelling, foul-tasting or all three, and served to make the victim feel so bad that when the effects of the medicine wore off they felt positively cured. There seem to have been two main choices: cajole a surgeon into coming along or risk the tender mercies of one's colleagues, hopefully guided by the information provided in some sort of handy home guide to medicating the unwell.

Quite a few surgeons went on expeditions, and because many of them liked to collect specimens, they often served two purposes: medical and scientific. Surgeons in those days were expected to be scientifically inclined, and when Allan Cunningham collected the first frill-necked lizard in 1820, it ended up in the collections of the Royal College of Surgeons.

George Bass was not only a surgeon but also a full partner in his explorations with Flinders, and John Harris seems to have been a willing participant in several expeditions. King, however, found himself without a medical man, and regretting it, in February 1818.

On rounding Cape Leeuwin, our crew were attacked with a bowel complaint, and symptoms of dysentery; the want of a surgeon to our establishment was most anxiously felt, from the fear that, by an unskilful or improper use of medicines, I might increase, instead of lessen the progress of complaints, which from the fatigues of such a service, in so warm a climate and in the unhealthy season, threatened to be frequent and severe. One or two of the people had complained of this disorder before we left Oyster Harbour, but it was not until we had sailed, that it assumed any serious appearance. After two days it happily began to subside, or I should of necessity have been obliged to resort to some place for relief, for we had, at one time, only four seamen to keep watch.

If a land party was laid low by illness or injury, they had a number of choices, including strapping the patient on a horse or camel and making haste, or stopping. At a pinch, one or two walking members could care for the rest of a party staggering home. But on a ship or boat, there was a minimum number of able hands needed to hoist and lower the sails, or to reset them when the wind came from another quarter, or when the ship went about onto another tack.

A number of French ships, in particular, had crewing problems while off the Australian coast, and so we can understand King's elation in May 1820 when he managed to acquire the services of a naval surgeon.

The accession of a surgeon to our small party relieved me of a greater weight of anxiety than I can describe; and when it is considered that Mr. Hunter left an employment of a much more lucrative nature to join an arduous service in a vessel whose only cabin was scarcely large enough to contain our mess-table, and which afforded neither comfort nor convenience of any description, I may be allowed here to acknowledge my thanks for the sacrifice he made.

James Hunter had just arrived in Australia after supervising the health of convicts on a transport, and obviously wanted more interesting work, but by the end of the year he had been replaced by another transport's surgeon, Andrew Montgomery.

When midshipman Roe fell 50 feet (15 metres) to the deck in June 1821, the work of Montgomery, aided by a naval surgeon from another ship, combined no doubt with Roe's good luck, brought him back to health and left him alive for later land-based work in Western Australia. This was the same Montgomery who had later to direct his shipmates as they removed a spear from his back.

There may, of course, have been fatal incidents that we never heard about, but as a rule the explorers seem to have been a lucky bunch. Peter Warburton reported being once struck at by a snake, but he said later that being half-starved gave him an unlikely benefit.

Had a narrow escape from a snake bite last night. Whilst walking from the camp fire to my rug I saw the reptile clearly in the moonlight, but not in time to alter my stride, and trod upon it about six inches above the tail. It turned upon me, of course, but whether it bit my trousers or not I don't know; if it did I derived some advantage from my extra thinness, as it could not find the leg inside them.

Warburton's Afghan camel driver, Sahleh, had less luck. Warburton said the scorpions were so common as to prevent them going about barefoot. He wrote that Sahleh claimed to be 'a professed Oriental snake charmer, and declares he can handle snakes and scorpions with impunity'; in spite of this, Sahleh had lost the use of one hand and arm after the sting of a scorpion. At that time it was largely a matter for Warburton's amusement, but six days later it was serious. 'If it continues to get worse, without any prospect of surgical aid, some one—not I—will have to chop his finger off with a tomahawk, or he will lose his arm and his life.' If only Mr Horrocks had taken a companion with equal good sense!

Two days later, on 2 January, the party had been relieved after the stronger members had pushed on to a nearby station and returned with help, but Sahleh was still in a bad way: 'Sahleh's finger looks very angry indeed; he may escape the tomahawk, but can hardly be spared the knife,' said Warburton. But Sahleh's fate is found in the closing notes to his journal, written the following May:

We have all got through our trials better than we could have expected. I believe my son and myself are the only two European sufferers. I have lost the sight of one eye, and my son is much shaken in his health. Sahleh, the Affghan, left his finger in Roebourne. Beyond this I know of no harm that has been done.

Aside from venomous animals and crocodiles, Australian explorers were really only at risk from their domestic animals like Harry the camel and horses that shied or bolted nervously at the wrong time. Curiously, the two main fears of modern tourists in Australia, sharks and dingoes, caused no real problems for the explorers, even though they expressed more than a little nervousness about them. Many managed to hook and land sharks of a significant size, a few complained about sharks driving away other fish or breaking their hooks, but no explorer was ever taken by a shark, so far as we know, though in 1818 Lieutenant King ate a crab they retrieved from the maw of a shark they had caught.

As for wild dogs, Cunningham, Oxley and Carron ate dingo, and Stokes shot one, mistaking it for a kangaroo. On Cape York, Carron complained of 'native dogs' rushing their sheep and scattering them, but these appear to have been dogs that travelled with the local Aborigines. He later killed and ate a kangaroo dog that was too weak to catch any more food for his ungrateful owners. Francis Gregory mentioned failing to get at a lair with pups in it, which sounds like a hunting attempt.

Burke reported feeling giddy after eating a snake, Warburton complained that they could not catch any snakes to eat, and

Carnegie reported eating a carpet snake with no ill effects. One way or another, it appears that the fearsome animals of Australia did the explorers more good than harm.

✝

TROUBLE WITH HORSES

Overseas tourists are reassured today that the animal involved in most deaths each year in Australia is the horse. The number of horse-related deaths is usually given as 'about twenty', but the figure used to be higher. Leichhardt wrote that Roper was hurt when he seized the tail of a horse to stop it. According to Leichhardt, this was their usual practice, but on this occasion the horse took exception to having its tail pulled and caught Roper in the chest with both of its rear hooves.

At the start of Stuart's successful crossing of Australia, one of the horses became anxious because a rope was choking it. When Stuart moved in to cut the rope, the horse reared and struck him on the temple with its hoof, knocking him senseless. It then stepped forward, placing a hind foot on Stuart's right hand and reared again, dislocating two joints of the first finger and ripping the nail from it. They bred them tough in those days, and Stuart continued on, but a year later he confided in his journal that his right hand remained 'nearly useless'.

Giles was very proud of his boots, the same ones he used to bail water, and he survived drinking from them. Then they became dangerous in an entirely unexpected way. He had repaired them 'with sixty horseshoe nails to each boot, all beautifully clenched within', making 'perfect dreadnoughts' of them, but they were nearly the death of him a few weeks later. He was bringing the horses into camp one morning, riding a rather skittish colt called Diaway. The horse was scared by something and fell and rolled, leaving Giles flat on his back but with one boot caught in the offside stirrup.

On my feet were those wonderful boots before described, with the sixty horseshoe nails in each, and it was no wonder that one of my feet got caught in the stirrup on the off side of the horse. It is one of the most horrible positions that the mind can well imagine, to contemplate being dragged by a horse. I have been dragged before now, and only escaped by miracles on each occasion. In this case, Diaway, finding me attached to him, commenced to lash out his newly shod heels at me, bounding away at the same time into a dense thicket of scrub close by ... The continual kickings I received—some on my legs and body, but mostly upon that portion of the frame which it is considered equally indecorous to present either to a friend or an enemy—at length bent one or two of the nail-heads which held me, and, tearing the upper leather off my boot, which fortunately was old, ripped it off, leaving me at length free.

But if the horses played up now and then, perhaps they should be forgiven, because most of the animals had but a single fate: to be worked until they were ready to drop, and then be killed and eaten. Diaway survived to be sold, rather than being eaten. Like the other successful explorers, Giles was not fastidious about what he ate, so we must assume he had a genuine fondness for Diaway—or maybe he thought the horse would be too tough.

✝

GUN INJURIES

Loaded guns, particularly the rather unsophisticated muzzle-loaders of the early nineteenth century, were always a risk, especially as men crowded into boats to visit a strange shore where their landing might attract a shower of spears and stones.

Aside from Horrocks' mishap with Harry the camel, the master of the *Beagle*, Alexander Usborne, was accidentally shot while in a boat, while Lieutenant Graham Gore of the *Beagle* was injured when his fowling piece burst while the lieutenant was attempting to bring down some birds for dinner. His comrades washed his wounded hand in brandy and bound it up, then, on his insistence, they continued their expedition. Lewis Fitzmaurice, one of the *Beagle*'s mates, was later shot in the ankle by yet another accidental discharge.

Robert Flood, Charles Sturt's stockman, was injured when a gun discharged while he was reloading at full gallop, hunting some wild cattle. He lost the first joints of three fingers on his right hand.

Gore was lucky to have his wound disinfected with brandy, but any good surgeon would have done the same. Standard medical histories would have us believe that before the 1860s nobody had any notion of germs, yet plenty of surgeons saw their patients recover after they applied various antiseptics such as brandy. And as we have seen, John Harris saved at least two men who were speared, and we might reasonably expect that he also used alcohol or other spirits to treat the wound.

Charlie Stansmore, one of Carnegie's party, died when he slipped on rocks and his loaded gun discharged directly into his heart. While Carnegie carried medicinal brandy, it could do nothing for Charlie.

BARCOO ROT AND BUSH CURES

The disease called scurvy at sea became Barcoo rot when it was encountered in the inland, though even at the end of the nineteenth century it seems few realized they were actually one and the same disease, going on a comment from David Carnegie.

Dave Wilson thought it unwise to come because his health was poor and his blood completely out of order, as evinced by the painful sores due to what is termed 'the Barcoo Rot.' This disease is very common in the bush, where no vegetables or change of food can be obtained, and must be something akin to scurvy. It is usually accompanied by retching and vomiting following every attempt to eat.

By the 1890s, scurvy was a rarity at sea, but the First Fleeters knew what they were dealing with when scurvy broke out in Sydney in May 1788. At that time, Watkin Tench complained that there were no suitable 'esculent vegetable productions' in the area, while none of the seeds planted had yet produced any vegetables.

Sturt had an excellent team on his final trip. John McDouall Stuart was his draughtsman and John Harris Browne (no relation to John Harris), a thorough bushman and an excellent surgeon, came along as a friend. When you read Sturt's account of their travels in dreadful conditions, you get the distinct impression they were a bunch of worthy men who knew what they were doing.

In 1845, Browne had no problem diagnosing Charles Sturt's condition as scurvy when his leader mentioned having a sore mouth and spongy gums. Browne and Poole, another of the officers in Sturt's party, were also troubled by scurvy, but Sturt's comments at the time reveal his ignorance about the true cause, a dietary deficiency. He stressed that he was moderate in his diet, but then noted that the likely reason the officers suffered from scurvy was that they tended to be out on expeditions away from the base camp much of the time, and eating bacon, while the underlings generally made only every second trip. This, he said, meant they were located more often at the base camp, and so ate fresh mutton more often. Browne, however, noticed that the locals were eating a small 'acid berry', and brought a bunch back to Sturt, who ate some of them and found his health improved.

John McDouall Stuart often ate pigface, a succulent plant that he hoped would prevent scurvy, and he also ate marsupial mice and crows ('very agreeable to taste and stomach', he called them). But if the explorers only had access to what seem like deficient medical treatments, their case was no worse than that of others in the bush. Soon after Charlie Stansmore's death, Carnegie was in the goldrush town of Halls Creek, when a 'poor chap' came in seeking help for scurvy. He was, said Carnegie, very ill indeed, and he then proposed a rather silly remedy.

> I happened to be up at the hospital, and asked the orderly [there was no doctor] what he would do for him in the way of nourishing food. 'Well,' said he, looking very wise, 'I think a little salt beef will meet the case.' And such would indeed have been his diet if I had not luckily had some Liebig's Extract; for the town was in a state verging on famine, dependent as it is on the whims of 'packers' and teamsters, who bring provisions from the coast, nearly three hundred miles, by road. Twice a year waggons arrive; for the rest everything is brought per

horseback, and when the rains are on, and the rivers running, their load is as often as not considerably damaged by immersion in the water.

Several of Carnegie's party (including Stansmore) had suffered badly from scurvy in the month before they arrived at Halls Creek, and seem not to have benefited from Liebig's Extract, a product still sold today as Oxo. It was, however, about all the medicine that was on offer. According to Carnegie, even the best liquor in such a place was bound to be concocted from 'red-pepper, kerosene, tobacco, methylated spirits, and what not'.

Under many circumstances, any vile fluid would be regarded as the perfect remedy for all conceivable ills. It would certainly be no worse than Stockholm tar, a mixture of phenols distilled from Swedish pine roots, and equally suited for curing boils or burns, tarring rigging or treating an injured hoof or a sheep that was nicked by the shears. Today, it is regarded as a dangerous substance that should not come in contact with the skin (it has even been banned in the European Union), but back then it was probably one of the less dangerous items in the explorer's medicine box. Nothing in the box could possibly have offered any respite, though, from the buzzing, crawling, whining and stinging pests of the desert, the plains, the coast, the swamps and the bush in general.

✝

THE FEAR OF
FLYING THINGS

Insects were the worst aspect of Australia, people said, complaining about the ubiquitous flies—and even in the city, flies were common in the unhygienic nineteenth century. Tropical accounts always included harrowing tales of green tree ants raining down from chopped trees, but the strongest invective was retained for mosquitoes. Even the ladylike Mrs Meredith, who had published delicate poetry in Britain, hated the mosquitoes around her house at Homebush (now a suburb of Sydney) more than the flies, of which she said:

> ... they swarm in every room in tens of thousands, and blacken the breakfast or dinner table as soon as the viands appear, tumbling into the cream, tea, wine, and gravy with the most disgusting familiarity. But worse than these are the mosquitoes, nearly as numerous, and infinitely more detestable to those for whose luckless bodies they form an attachment, as they do to most new comers; a kind of initiatory compliment which I would gladly dispense with, for most intolerable is the torment they cause in the violent irritation of their mountainous bites.

In her day, Homebush was a lonely spot on the Parramatta Road, infested with rogues and bushrangers. In today's more civilized world, the numbers of flies and mosquitoes have been reduced, and the rogues and bushrangers have been replaced by used-car yards. Captain Stokes would have considered this an improvement—he rated the flies and mosquitoes as almost equally evil, but in the end granted the mosquitoes a points win.

> We found constant occasion, when on shore, to complain of this fly nuisance; and when combined with their allies, the mosquitoes, no human endurance could, with any patience, submit to the trial. The flies are at you all day, crawling into your eyes, up your nostrils, and down your throat, with the most irresistible perseverance; and no sooner do they, from sheer exhaustion, or the loss of daylight, give up the attack, than they are relieved by the musquitos, who completely exhaust the patience which their predecessors have so severely tried. It may seem absurd to my readers to dwell upon such a subject; but those, who, like myself, have been half-blinded, and to boot, almost stung to death, will not wonder, that even at this distance of time and place, I recur with disgust to the recollection.

A little later, Stokes outlined his remedy for mosquitoes: Mackintosh leggings, which he called 'encumbrances not desirable for a pedestrian with the thermometer at 87 degrees, particularly when worn over a pair of Flushing trousers', and especially when finished off with 'the additional security afforded by a large painted coat'.

Looking back, the history of explorer–mosquito conflict begins with Joseph Banks calling them troublesome at Botany Bay, and Watkin Tench spoke less than kindly of them. But many of the explorers behaved in irrational ways in response to the mosquitoes. By 1819, Phillip Parker King was experiencing the mosquitoes of the northern coast.

> Our fears of being attacked by the natives being now dispelled, our party composed themselves again to rest, but without obtaining any sleep in consequence of the immense swarms of mosquitoes, which buzzing about in incredible numbers were not to be kept from stinging us by any measures we could devize. The tent was very soon deserted and many other places were tried in vain; the only method at all successful, by which some respite was obtained, was by lying upon the ground within two feet of the blaze of the fire; the heat and smoke of which, with the danger of our clothes catching fire, were insignificant inconveniences compared with the mosquitoes' stings; and those only who placed themselves in this situation obtained a few hours' sleep.

And a few years later, here is Charles Sturt, on his first journey, out near the Darling River in western New South Wales with Hamilton

Hume. They had gone too far out from their base camp to get back that night, so they looked for and found water, then tethered their horses:

> ... and should have been tolerably comfortable, had not the mosquitoes been so extremely troublesome. They defied the power of smoke, and annoyed me so much, that, hot as it was, I rolled myself in my boat cloak, and perspired in consequence to such a degree, that my clothes were wet through, and I had to stand at the fire in the morning to dry them. Mr. Hume, who could not bear such confinement, suffered the penalty, and was most unmercifully bitten.

John Stokes, however, seems to have been the champion of telling stories of mosquitoes, in this case swarms encountered while HMS *Beagle* was working along Australia's tropical coasts. Mapping meant getting right in close and venturing deep into the mangroves.

> I noticed one man dressed as if in the frozen north, hold his bag over the fire till it was quite full of smoke, and then get into it, a companion securing the mouth over his head at the apparent risk of suffocation; he obtained three hours of what he gratefully termed comfortable sleep, but when he emerged from his shelter, where he had been stewed up with the thermometer at 87 degrees, his appearance may be easily imagined ... One

poor fellow, whose patience was quite exhausted, fairly jumped
into the river to escape further persecution.

Flies and mosquitoes were, and remain, a problem for those
working with complicated navigational, surveying or scientific
equipment, where the user needs to remain completely still while
using both hands to take a reading. For such people, a fly veil of
some sort is truly a necessity, but until such a device was invented
the flies made explorers miserable. It may be a myth, but those who
have experienced the conditions are willing to believe in the
'Bedourie fly veil'. This apparently involved smearing a shirt-tail
lightly with excrement and leaving it hanging out to attract flies
away from the head, and specifically, away from the eyes, ears,
nose and mouth.

SANDY BLIGHT IN THE
OPHTHALMIA RANGE

The flies, seen only as a ghastly annoyance, actually represented one
of the deadliest risks to humans, because they spread trachoma.
Known colloquially as 'sandy blight', this is an infection of the eyes,
a form of conjunctivitis caused by a small organism called *Chlamydia
trachomatis*. The infection can lead to secondary bacterial infections

that may cause blindness. The condition was recorded in Egypt in about 1900 BC, and was known to the founder of Greek medicine, Hippocrates. Yet while it was long recognized as contagious, nobody seems to have realized that it is spread by flies.

Today, trachoma is still the third most common cause of human blindness, even though the organism was identified in 1907, and shown to be the cause of trachoma when a blind volunteer's eyes were inoculated with the bacterium in 1957. Many early visitors to the Australian north coast commented on the clouds of flies and the incidence of blindness in the local population, but the penny seems not to have dropped. Other supposed causes appealed more.

In February 1818, Allan Cunningham had seen trachoma on the north-west coast and referred to Aborigines' eyes as 'affected much with watery humours, occasioned by their habits of sitting over the smokes of their little fires'. His companion King, on the other hand, noted the following year that 'the greater part of the crew were affected with ophthalmia, probably occasioned by the excessive glare and reflection of the sun's rays from the calm glassy surface of the sea'. John Lort Stokes was closer to the money in 1839.

> We had both suffered much inconvenience from the attacks of flies upon our visual organs, necessarily exposed and undefended as they had been when we were occupied during the observations and in viewing the strange scenes of the last eighteen days. The irritation upon the lids produced a copious

discharge, which fairly sealed them up at night; so that, at last, in order to have them ready for immediate use, I found it requisite to sleep with a wet linen cloth covering each eye.

In 1845, Charles Sturt seemed to be on the right track as well, referring to his men complaining of disordered bowels and sore eyes, 'but I attributed both to the weather, and to the annoyance of the flies and mosquitos'. In the following year, he noted blindness in the Aborigines: 'many had lost an eye by inflammation from the attacks of flies'.

In 1859, though, Stuart complained, 'My eyes very bad from the effects of the glare of the sun on the sandhills, and the heat reflected from them, and that everlasting torment, the flies', showing that once again environment was gaining ground as the likely cause, but this was at almost the exact time that a few brave scientists scattered across Europe were offering the daring and outrageous theory that disease was caused by very small organisms, even if all the best authorities pointed to other causes.

Here is a typical comment from Ernest Giles: 'Everybody had an attack of the blight, as ophthalmia is called in Australia, which with the flies were enough to set any one deranged.' A week or so later, in June 1876, he wrote, 'Since my last attack of ophthalmia, I suffer great pain and confusion when using the sextant. The attack I have mentioned in this journey was by no means the only one I have had on my numerous journeys; I have indeed had more or less virulent attacks for the last twenty years, and I believe the disease is now chronic, though suppressed.'

At the start of his 1876 infection, mentioned above, Giles wrote of how the party 'enjoyed the rain exceedingly, except that our senses of enjoyment were somewhat blunted, for all of us had been attacked with ophthalmia for several days previously. Livingstone remarks in one of his works that, in Africa, attacks of ophthalmia generally precede rain.'

In general, this dangerous condition was attributed to other desert conditions and climate, so we find David Carnegie writing: 'Besides these small troubles, Breaden and Godfrey were suffering agonies from "sandy blight," a sort of ophthalmia, which is made almost unbearable by the clouds of flies, the heat, the glare, and the dust.'

Indeed, it seems almost to have been regarded as a joke. As a result of that 1876 infection, Giles named a range of mountains the Ophthalmia Range 'in consequence of my suffering so much from that frightful malady'. All the same, he was unhappy about it, noting, 'I could not take any observations, and I cannot be very certain where this range lies.' These days, most people remain uncertain of its whereabouts as well, even if they can locate Mount Newman, which is part of the range.

✟

11.

What they learned or achieved

WHILE THERE WERE MANY FOIBLES, follies and lucky escapes, the people we call the explorers did a good job of surveying the land. They drew maps, identified the plants and animals, found negotiable paths, located water and pastoral land and, for the most part, remained friendly with the local inhabitants. They were the true pioneers of Australia.

MAKING ROADS

The incidental results of the explorers' travels were more clearly marked trails and a few reports, but soon the official mapmakers overtook them, trudging along with chain and theodolite, laying down base lines and establishing a framework of landmarks. However, even the surveyors needed good bushmen, either Aboriginal or white, in their party, people who understood what the bush was about and what worked out there.

Where cattle and sheep can go, so can railway lines, and where cattle and sheep and people are found, so there was a need for a railway. The routes laid down by the explorers, following Aboriginal paths, became the major transport arteries of the nineteenth and twentieth centuries. Parts have since been straightened out by brute force, explosives and bulldozers, but now tourists can criss-cross the continent, largely following the ancient routes.

We have people like Francis Birtles to thank for making it easier. Born in 1882, Birtles served in the Boer War before returning to Australia, where he set out in 1907 to bicycle 'around Australia', which meant Sydney to Brisbane to Charters Towers to Darwin to Alice Springs, Adelaide, Melbourne and Sydney. Hobart missed out for obvious reasons, but Perth was not left out for long.

When Birtles died in 1941, his grave at Waverley cemetery was marked: 'Francis Birtles, explorer and photographer'. In one sense, he was a pioneer, following marked routes in a new way, and given that the 'real' explorers also followed ancient foot tracks, perhaps we can allow him to claim the designation of 'explorer'. Like his predecessors, he lived off the land, and photographs show his bicycle fitted with a holster that carried his trusty hunting rifle. Unlike his predecessors, he was able to harvest rabbits for much of the trip.

His first trip took twelve months, but in the following year he cycled from Perth to Sydney in just 44 days. Then, having seen what the route was like, he set out in 1912 to make the journey in a car with a wooden axle. He chose timber for the axle so he could make another from local materials when it broke—which it did, and he did! Roads and railways were beginning to fill in the gaps, with steamers working their way around the periphery, and within a decade people were beginning to look ahead to air travel that today allows us to fly effortlessly over the desert wastes where, a century earlier, pioneers slogged. On the bitumen roads of modern Australia, motorists can cover a degree of latitude or longitude in an hour, when explorers would take three to seven days, sometimes more, to make the same progress. For us, there are no barriers, because where we cannot get through, we can go around, or over.

TO PASS THE
IMPASSABLE BARRIER

Every explorer came up against barriers to progress, especially explorers using carts and drays, but the first 25 years of European settlement were contained by a supposedly impassable barrier in the form of the Blue Mountains. The story of Blaxland, Wentworth and

Lawson, and their 'brilliant idea' of keeping on the ridges has been taught to generations of schoolchildren by generations of teachers lacking any bush experience. They deserve no special credit, because any hill walker, any person living in a mountainous area, anywhere in the world, knew that the trick was to follow the ridges. This simple fact remains obvious today.

Sit beneath any mountain or hill and trace with your eye the best path to take you as high as possible, and you will track the way that goes up a ridge. Look for where the vegetation is thinnest in bush that was last burned a few years back, and you will find it on the ridges. Even without 'native roads' to follow, or information from Aborigines or errant convicts, the ridge route is the obvious one, just as soon as a few carts have struggled into ravines and over the tumbled rocks only to be met with cliffs.

Eyre had tried to push north, past the Flinders Range in South Australia but, each time, came to a salt lake or saw one ahead of him. These barriers were, he said, 80 to 90 miles (128 to 144 kilometres) apart, and they all had the same appearance. More importantly, he looked down from Mount Serle at the northern end of the range, and he could see drainage channels radiating out in all directions, feeding into what appeared, from a distance, to be a continuous horseshoe shape of boggy salt lake. The channels were marked by the trees that lined them, and where an ending could be seen it was always the dazzling white of a salt lake.

We know now that there were gaps between—that Lake Torrens, as Eyre conceived it, was really a series of lakes—but the depressing vista of an apparently impenetrable barrier to the north persuaded Eyre to head first south and then westward, in the hope that he might find a way leading to the north, somewhere along the Great Australian Bight.

In other cases, the barriers were scrub that blocked horses and men or, when it gave way, tore ferociously at them. William Carron reported that Kennedy's party could make at best 3 to 5 miles (5 to 8 kilometres) a day as they attacked Cape York.

> We were compelled to cut away the scrub, and the banks of some of the creeks, before we were able to cross them, and frequently obliged to run a creek up and down some distance before we could find a place where it was passable at all.

Other explorers complained of losses due to ripping and damage as well. 'We had lost about 143 pounds of flour; Mr. Gilbert lost his tent, and injured the stock of his gun,' wrote Leichhardt. Stuart also suffered the loss of flour, and had to stop to repair torn saddlebags, ripped as the horses pushed through thick scrub. Even their clothes suffered: 'We are all nearly naked, the scrub has been so severe on our clothes; one can scarcely tell the original colour of a single garment, everything is so patched.'

Then there were the endless lines of sand ridges that drove the explorers to distraction. Coming at the end of the era, David Carnegie had his predecessors as style guides, but still did well.

A vast, howling wilderness of high, spinifex-clad ridges of red sand, so close together that in a day's march we crossed from sixty to eighty ridges, so steep that often the camels had to crest them on their knees, and so barren and destitute of vegetation [saving spinifex] that one marvels how even camels could pick up a living.

✝

PRESERVING THE RECORD

Mostly, the explorers needed to be the authors of their own success, literally, by polishing their records and setting them before an admiring public, courtesy of a publisher somewhere. There seems almost to have been a formula for these works: many chapters; details of all the strange things seen; maps, charts and figures; a few adventures and privations; and—since the work would sell mainly in a market that identified itself as British (even in Australia)—as many celebrations per page as possible of the absolute perfection of the British explorer, his religion, his culture, his forbearance in the face of ungrateful, deceitful, sullen natives, his wit, charm and ability to extricate himself from danger, vicious animals, vile weather; and a bit on the quaint savages and their heathen habits.

No single journal contains all of these elements, but even so they usually make quite good reading. Ernest Giles' is perhaps the best, although the matter-of-fact accounts of King, Cunningham, Oxley and Eyre are excellent. Many are brief daily accounts, but most show signs of extensive reworking to improve the interest level for a market that must have been close to flooded. Some of these have only ever seen the light of day by reproduction in works like the *Historical Records of New South Wales* and a few specialist journals like the *Journal of the Royal Geographical Society*. There is one standout among the journals: the accounts of Augustus Gregory are masterpieces of restraint, as we can see in the following deadpan account.

> ... the water was running strong twenty yards, and one to two feet deep; in examining the ford my horse trod on the back of a large alligator, which seemed to be equally astonished as the horse at this unexpected meeting; I then proceeded up the river a mile and a half and halted ...

Carnegie and Giles would both have made far more of that encounter. So would the first person to burst into print on Australia, William Dampier. He provided brief but interesting details to a ready audience, but before him most 'discoveries' were regarded as commercial-in-confidence, with tight security applied to stop any literate crewman making unauthorized notes, and this again became the rule later on.

Those who combined a bit of luck, wit, preparation and training generally got more credit, but it seems those with a flair for catching the imagination fared best of all. That is the only explanation for Augustus Gregory being unknown today. If he had been able to get a bit more worked up about that crocodile that his horse trod on, perhaps he would also have made it into the school textbooks.

James Cook had Admiralty instructions to hand his journal over to a London writer and editor named Dr John Hawkesworth, so this hack could primp the plain-spoken sailor's prose into what Cook's biographer Alan Villiers calls with a justifiable irony 'something really readable—some of it mincing, paltry puffed-up stuff, fit for the eighteenth century'.

Hawkesworth added material from Banks' journal, some of it ill-considered criticism of St Helena, so when Cook revisited the island on his second voyage, the locals asked in some outrage why his book said there were no wheeled vehicles or wheelbarrows there. In vain did he protest his innocence, for his name was there on the title page. Each morning while he was on the island, he would awake to find most of the island's wheeled vehicles and all the island wheelbarrows parked outside his door, drawn up for inspection, as it were.

Even more annoying was the pirate account of the voyages brought out anonymously before Cook's 'own' (that is, Hawkesworth's) version. Cook and others believed the culprit to be none other than James Matra (often referred to as Magra), a midshipman described by Cook in his manuscript journal of the first voyage (it was edited out of the 1893 published version) as 'good for nothing'.

The First Fleet seems not to have been under any such restrictions, and any number of journals were produced, though some of them have only been printed in comparatively recent times. The curtain came down with the wars against Napoleon, and in March 1801 we find Governor King instructing James Grant:

> Previous to your arrival in this port, on your return you are to demand from the officers and ship's company the journals or any other remarks, drawings, or sketches that may have been made during the voyage. These, together with your own original journals, in which your proceedings of all kinds have been minuted, and the plans, charts, drawings, and sketches you have made, tending to illustrate the hydrography, geography, or natural history of the country, all which journals and drawings are to be sealed up by you, to be delivered to me on your arrival in this harbour; and all such seeds of plants, trees and shrubs, and specimens of animals, vegetables, and minerals, such articles of the dresses and arms of the natives as you shall think worthy the notice of His Majesty's Ministers or the Royal Society, to be transmitted by me to them. For all which this shall be your authority.

In April 1801, Robert Brown, naturalist; William Westall, landscape and figure draughtsman; Ferdinand Bauer, botanic draughtsman; Peter Good, gardener; and John Allen, miner; all signed a solemn undertaking, imposed by the Lords of the

Admiralty, that after their travels with Flinders, 'all journals, remarks, memorandums, drawings, scetches, collections of natural history, and habits, arms, utensils, armaments, &c., of every kind ... ' would be handed over to the Admiralty on their return.

Provided the men had been of good behaviour on the voyage, their lordships proposed to publish a narrative of the voyage, and the scientific assistants would be allowed a share of the profits. After that was done, the choicest of the specimens would be distributed as their lordships saw fit, and the remainder would go back to the assistants.

In short, 'the remainder of the descriptions of plants and animals, &c., and the scetches of all kinds, shall be at the disposal of the persons who have made them, for the purpose of being publish'd by them whenever it is thought proper, and at their own risque and for their own advantage ... ' The rules laid down that only those of the assistants who had been harmonious, of good behaviour and humour during the voyage would be allowed to share in the division of the spoils. There were also dark hints about punishment, enough stick-and-carrot to ensure that all collections were enthusiastically prepared, added to and maintained.

There remained the risk of records and collections being lost to shipwreck, so care had to be taken to make the results secure against loss through misfortune. Thus we find Lieutenant King being told by the Admiralty:

You will take care to make duplicate copies of all your notes, surveys, and drawings; and you are to take every possible

opportunity of transmitting one copy to the Earl of Bathurst,
and the other to me for their Lordship's information; but you
need not send duplicates by the same conveyance.

In other words, spread the risk over several ships. Perhaps
making copies was what they did in their leisure time. Certainly
King had Roe hard at it in 1821, because he mentioned arriving at
Mauritius, where three reduced copies of charts of the north-west
coast and a brief account of their voyage were handed over to
HM Sloop *Cygnet*, for delivery to the Admiralty.

Journals were prized, whether they were the explorer's own or
somebody else's published account. Eyre's tale of his epic journey to
King George's Sound is one of continually lightening the load,
leaving behind those items that could no longer be justified
or carried. Some items were buried, in case he needed to come
back to them, others were merely discarded, while treasures
were retained.

At the end of March 1841, Eyre needed to lighten the load
on his pack animals and, with Baxter, he went through their
possessions, discarding pack-saddles, most of the spare horseshoes,
the water kegs, clothes, some of the firearms, the medicines, and
even, though it irked him, a copy of Captain Sturt's *Expeditions* that
had been personally given to him by Sturt.

... it was the last kind offering of friendship from a highly
esteemed friend, and nothing but necessity would have induced

me to part with it. Could the donor, however, have seen the miserable plight we were reduced to, he would have pitied and forgiven an act that circumstances alone compelled me to.

Eyre undertook two more rounds of jettisoning in April: one before John Baxter was killed, and then in late June, estimating he had ten days' travel left to reach Albany, Eyre went through a further refining of what needed to be carried, and finally abandoned his horses just before they crossed the last river on their way into Albany. He also left the remaining baggage, clothes, spare shoes, medicines, saddles, horseshoes and ammunition, taking only his own journals and charts. Those alone could not be abandoned.

Then having 'turned our horses loose, and piled up our baggage, now again greatly reduced, I took my journals and charts, and with Wylie forded the river about breast high'. They trudged through rain that would have been welcome for much of the journey, and reached the town with the precious records of their travels and travails.

That most amateur of explorers, John Horrocks, kept a journal of sorts, telling of daily experiences, but providing very little benefit to those who came after. He took the artist S.T. Gill with him, and complained from time to time that Gill had delayed him, yet it is Gill who has brought Horrocks most delightfully to life with his paintings, showing his leader always equipped with a map case slung behind him. Then Harry the camel shot him and Horrocks realized in the South Australian arid zone that he was mortal, and that his expedition was defunct.

That other total amateur, Robert O'Hara Burke, was given clear instructions about records: 'You will cause full reports to be furnished by your officers on any subject of interest, and forward them to Melbourne as often as may be practicable without retarding the progress of the expedition.'

The highly professional Stuart must have wished he had a map case slung behind him at all times, like Horrocks. In January 1860, he complained that his men had been at the maps.

> Very much annoyed by the misconduct of the two men I left behind at the camp; they have had the impertinence to open my plan-case, and have so damaged my principal plan with their hot moist hands, that I know not what to do with it. This is not the first time they have done it.

It may not have been entirely a matter of curiosity that led the men to examine the maps in this way, given a comment Stuart made when explaining why he had not provided full details of his proposed route for the Overland Telegraph line.

> I should have been glad for this information to have accompanied my works, but I find I cannot postpone them longer for that purpose, as parties have already taken advantage of the delay occasioned by my illness at the time of, and since,

my arrival home to collect what scraps of information they could obtain, with the intention of publishing them as my travels. I leave the reward of such conduct to a discriminating public ...

A month later, though, a far more confident Francis Gregory noted on 21 July 'my own time being principally taken up in roughly plotting the country already explored, so as to secure all the information obtained, in the event of any accident occurring to my field-books'. Here, the most likely accident was not death, but a careering horse, an unforeseen blaze, a wild storm or flood that might expunge all the information from the pages of field books kept handy for notes to be made.

In 1875, Ernest Giles suffered the sort of accident Francis Gregory had feared.

While we were at dinner to-day a sudden whirl-wind sprang up and sent a lot of my loose papers, from where I had been writing, careering so wildly into the air, that I was in great consternation lest I should lose several sheets of my journal, and find my imagination put to the test of inventing a new one. We all ran about after the papers, and so did some of the blacks, and finally they were all recovered.

✝

SURVIVING TO

CLAIM FAME

When Cook came through the Pacific, it was supposedly to allow his astronomers to observe the transit of Venus from Tahiti, but this scientific pursuit may well have been a cover for a more serious mission: looking for a southern land and southern naval bases.

With the astronomical work out of the way, Cook visited New Zealand and the east coast of Australia, where all went well at first. He had no way of knowing that the reefs are far from the coast in more southerly waters but begin to crowd the shore further up the Queensland coast. This meant danger was able to sneak up on Cook as he worked northward, and with little warning he found himself hemmed in between reefs and the shore. Within a few days, the *Endeavour* was holed.

Cook had veered away from the shore at night to avoid shoals, and found the reef in the dark, exchanging a known danger on shore for the hidden threat of the reefs. Banks told the story like this:

> At night fall rocks and sholes were seen ahead, on which the
> ship was put upon a wind off shore. While we were at supper she
> went over a bank of 7 or 8 fathom water which she came upon
> very suddenly; this we concluded to be the tail of the Sholes we

had seen at sunset and therefore went to bed in perfect security, but scarce were we warm in our beds when we were calld up with the alarming news of the ship being fast ashore upon a rock, which she in a few moments convincd us of by beating very violently against the rocks. Our situation became now greatly alarming: we had stood off shore 3 hours and a half with a plesant breeze so knew we could not be very near it: we were little less than certain that we were upon sunken coral rocks, the most dreadfull of all others on account of their sharp points and grinding quality which cut through a ships bottom almost immediately. The officers however behavd with inimitable coolness void of all hurry and confusion; a boat was got out in which the master went and after sounding round the ship found that she had ran over a rock and consequently had Shole water all round her.

Anchors were laid out to haul the ship off the rocks, ballast and six of the ship's guns were thrown overboard to help raise the *Endeavour*, but as the rocks or coral were no longer in the holes, water flowed in faster than the pumps could clear it. The boats were not enough to carry all the ship's company ashore to what they saw as a barren land with no food, and where they would lack the arms to defend themselves. If ever there was a time for despair, this was it.

Banks wrote that 'fear of Death now stard us in the face; hopes we had none but of being able to keep the ship afloat till we could run her ashore on some part of the main where out of her materials we might build a vessel large enough to carry us to the East Indies.' The solution was at hand, though, in the recollections of a midshipman. They needed simply to fother the bottom, he said. This meant hauling a prepared sail across the hole on the outside of the hull, stemming the inward-rushing torrent.

Cook later explained fothering (the 'Oacham', by the way, is oakum, unravelled old rope). Like Banks and Evans, Cook's spelling was peculiar, but Cook and Banks were well regarded by King George III, so nobody ever sniggered at them as they did at Evans.

> The Leak now decreaseth, but for fear it should break out again we got the Sail ready fill'd for fothering; the manner this is done is thus: We Mix Oacham and Wool together [but Oacham alone would do], and chop it up Small, and then stick it loosely by handfulls all over the Sail, and throw over it Sheep dung or other filth. Horse Dung for this purpose is the best. The Sail thus prepared is hauld under the Ship's bottom by ropes, and if the place of the Leak is uncertain, it must be hauld from one part of her bottom to another until one finds the place where it takes effect. While the Sail is under the Ship the Oacham, etc., is washed off, and part of it carried along with the water into the Leak, and in part stops up the hole. Mr. Monkhouse, one of my Midshipmen, was once in a Merchant Ship which Sprung a Leak, and made 48 Inches Water per hour; but by this means was brought home from Virginia to London with only

her proper crew; to him I gave the direction of this, who executed it very much to my satisfaction.

Banks was also impressed, and no doubt the crew were as well, from Banks' description of the period leading to the attempt: 'While this work was going on the water rather gaind on those who were pumping which made all hands impatient for the tryal.' As we know now, they got ashore in the Endeavour River near modern Cooktown, and repaired the ship. The end result was that instead of limping into Timor in a frail hull made of salvaged sticks, having abandoned all the scientific specimens and data, they reached England in triumph with their collections intact.

The effects of Cook's expedition were far-reaching. King George III was entertaining some thoughts on lightning conductors a few years later and quarrelled with the Royal Society, whose joint scientific opinion matched that of an American rebel called Benjamin Franklin. To patch up relations, the Royal Society appointed Joseph Banks (by now Sir Joseph, the king's favourite) as their next president, giving him a magnificent position of power from which to pursue his aim of creating a colony in Australia, at Botany Bay.

Matters could have been so very different. If Monkhouse had not known about fothering bottoms, or if the hole had been a bit larger, the ship would have gone down. And if the ship never got back to England, later expeditions might have tracked them as far as Tahiti, perhaps even to New Zealand, but to no real benefit, and with no additions to the charts of Australia's coastline. And until 1788, and even later, an accurate version of the coastline was what was needed to give landsmen something to fill in. History may be written by the victors, but it is generally about the survivors and the known dead who ventured into areas where the maps said no more than 'Here There Be Dragons'.

With or without dragons, it was dangerous. We cannot really imagine now how dangerous it was to sail in uncharted waters in a ship with a year's growth of animals and plants on its bottom. A ship in those days was an inelegant assembly of timbers, Stockholm tar and natural fibres with a few bits of metal, a hodge-podge destined to be pushed and shoved by conspiring currents, storms, tides, waves and winds, and left defenceless against those forces in unexpected calms.

Aside from growths on the surface that slowed the vessel, rot and worms ate into the timber itself. When King returned from his 1820 voyage, the *Mermaid* was surveyed: 'Upon stripping the copper off the bottom, the tide flowed into her, and proved that to the copper sheathing alone we were indebted for our safe return. The iron spikes that fastened her were entirely decayed ... '

It was risky enough to stand in towards the coast in temperate areas, but it was deadly dangerous in tropical waters, where coral teeth quite as fierce as any dragon's teeth were waiting to chomp into the hull, so unless there was some good reason to approach the coast, sailors did not do so. There might not be dragons as such, but there was no sense in testing what else was there, until there was a reason to do so.

Bougainville came close to Australia in June 1768, but he was just north of Cairns, at a latitude where he would have to thread his way through the Great Barrier Reef, and with no engine, no charts, no knowledge of what the winds or currents might do, he turned away, like a sensible sailor, and missed the chance to claim Australia, two years ahead of Cook.

The visit of La Pérouse to Botany Bay would never have made Australia a French possession, but if Bougainville had mapped and claimed Australia's east coast as Cook did, things might have turned out differently. The chasm between winning and losing is always a slim gap at the start.

12.

Winners and losers

THE WINNERS IN THE STORY OF MAPPING AUSTRALIA were those who had one or more of the following:

- a curiosity and a determination to go out and see what was to be found;
- the ability to plan a large-scale operation;
- the political skill to get together the necessary support and finance for an expedition;
- an understanding of the land and its inhabitants—animal, plant and human;
- the skills of navigation and mapping;
- the ability to lead humans, to console and persuade them when the going is tough;

- the ability to tell a good story; and above all,
- a good deal of luck.

The failures were those who missed out on perhaps just one of those, at a critical moment. If Stokes had been a slightly slower swimmer; if Giles' boots had been slightly larger or stronger; if one of Oxley's horses had fallen, coming down the mountains to Port Macquarie; if Roe had fallen to the deck at a different angle; if the Gregory brothers had gone to Canada instead of Australia—any of these would have changed the way Australia was mapped. If the party left behind by Burke and Wills had waited one more day for them, Burke would have survived to ride in triumph into Melbourne, he would have published his own journal, and Wills would have been reduced to a footnote.

EYRE AND WYLIE
ON THE BEACHES

There have been countless popular books about Burke and Wills, perhaps because they were so disastrous but, that aside, most explorers are remembered only by places and highways named after them; a plaque here or there, erected by a local historical society; and one or two pictures, clichéd into iconic status, like the engraving of

Kennedy being speared in the back (reinforcing the sense of 'native treachery') or the engraving of Eyre and Wylie walking along a beach on their way to King George's Sound (reproduced in this book opposite page 1) that has graced almost every schoolbook and work on the explorers that has appeared in the past century.

There are just two problems with the picture of Eyre and Wylie, which seems to date back to the 1880s. First, it fails to show the horses that they kept alive and used, right up to the last river before King George's Sound, where Eyre let them go rather than swim them over the river in his weakened state. We can forgive that error because the horses might have been, as we say in camera language, just out of shot, but the second error is a huge one. There can be no mistaking it, once you look: Eyre and Wylie are going the wrong way!

They are shown trudging along a beach, Wylie carrying a sack slung over his shoulder and a large billy, Eyre carrying a gun. They are ragged, Wylie lacks a shirt, and Eyre is shown gaining support from his hand on Wylie's shoulder. Their shadows point to the sea, as they would on a southern coast in the southern hemisphere, but the shadows and the sea are on the right, and that means they are going east, not west!

This image, in a variety of forms, seems to have decorated textbooks and other accounts of the explorers for the best part of a century. Some are coloured, suggesting that the work was painted at some stage. It is possible, though, that this was originally a painting, because it commonly happened that paintings were photographed and projected onto the engraver's plate. In this way, a copy was engraved with the same directional features, but when this was used to print copies they would have been mirror images of the original artwork. I further conjecture that the painting was engraved in Europe, where a person on a coast, with the sea and the shadow on the right, would indeed have been walking to the west.

It matters little. The picture exists in many forms, most Australians would recognize the subject of the illustration, and right way or wrong way, that portrait pushed the pair to stardom. What they did was an amazing feat, but very few Australians have ever followed the path Eyre and Wylie laid down, preferring an inland route instead.

KENNEDY'S MANY MISTAKES

In 1848, Edmund Kennedy embarked on an ill-conceived and ill-planned attempt to batter through rainforest and scramble over mountains with carts. It all fell apart when the carts had to be abandoned, but the expedition was ready to fail even before it started. In the end, very little was retrieved and nothing was achieved. They also left behind cross-cut saws, pickaxes and specimen boxes.

Looking at the Kennedy expedition, you get the distinct impression of a wounded beast lumbering along and spouting its life's blood. Kennedy had learned the brute-force military approach from Major Mitchell, but the tricks that worked on the western plains were less well suited to the rainforests of tropical Queensland. William Carron listed their equipment as follows:

> Our dry provisions comprized one ton of flour, ninety lbs. of tea, and six hundred lbs. of sugar. Besides these necessary supplies for subsistence on the road, we took with us twenty-four pack-saddles, one heavy square cart, two spring carts, with harness for nine horses, four tents, a canvas sheepfold, twenty-two pounds gunpowder, one hundred and thirty lbs. shot, a quarter cask of ammunition, twenty-eight tether ropes, each twenty-one yards long, forty hobble chains and straps, together with boxes, paper, &c., for preserving specimens, firearms, cloaks, blankets, tomahawks, and other minor requisites for such an expedition, not forgetting a supply of fish-hooks and other small articles, as presents for the natives.

One of the horses drowned before they could even get it ashore from the ship that carried them to Queensland. After a week ashore, the party set off, on 5 June 1848, with three horses on each cart. By 9 June, they had to stop for two days, while an advance party looked for a route for the carts; by 16 June, they were bogged down in swamps; and in early July, they were still in the swamps, the sheep were ill and two of the men had 'ague'. The carts had carried 700 pounds (317.5 kilograms) each, but by 14 July one of them was broken. All three were abandoned, with the equipment being shifted to the horses.

During August, the expedition progressively abandoned the horses as the animals became worn out. When one of the party, Luff, became too weak, they burned two tents and put him on the horse instead. Two days later they had to kill another horse. Then in late December came rescue from a ship-borne search party, but, as we have seen, Carron was less than grateful because his specimens had to be abandoned. Botanists value some things more than life.

BURKE AND WILLS:
A LACK OF EXPERIENCE

Burke and Wills, those two bumblers with the sensitivity, awareness and tact of a five-day-dead goanna, were cared for by their Aboriginal neighbours near the base that the back-up party had established (usually referred to as the DIG tree). Incidentally, if ever there was a need for evidence of the incompetence of the committee that set up what they called the Victorian Exploring Expedition (which we now call the Burke and Wills expedition), the following wildly optimistic instructions to Burke would surely provide it. The blind were not so much leading the blind, as standing behind them, shrieking advice and laying about them with whips. In effect, they were suggesting that the party travel from Melbourne to the Gulf of Carpentaria, then right across the continent as well. Either one would have been a challenge, yet they asked for both!

> Should you, however, fail in connecting the two points of Stuart's and Gregory's Farthest, or should you ascertain that this space has been already traversed, you are requested if possible to connect your explorations with those of the younger Gregory, in the vicinity of Mount Gould, and thence you might proceed to Sharks' Bay, or down the River Murchison, to the settlements in Western Australia.
>
> This country would afford the means of recruiting the strength of your party, and you might, after a delay of five or six months, be enabled, with the knowledge of the country you shall have previously acquired, to return by a more direct route through South Australia to Melbourne.
>
> If you should, however, have been successful in connecting Stuart's with Gregory's farthest point in 1856 [Mount Wilson], and your party should be equal to the task, you would probably find it possible from thence to reach the country discovered by the younger Gregory.

Leaving Menindie, Burke went one better than other explorers who got rid of supplies, as he also jettisoned half of his party, telling them to follow along behind to Cooper's Creek, after which the expedition would lumber along to the north coast. The following party dithered and delayed, and in the end, just four of the lead group (Burke, Wills, King and Gray) set off, lightly equipped. Now they were too lightly equipped, but even so they were forced to abandon more items on the way back down, as Wills explained in his notebook.

> On our way back, Rajah showed signs of being done up. He had been trembling greatly all the morning. On this account his load was further lightened to the amount of a few pounds by the doing away with the sugar, ginger, tea, cocoa, and two or three tin plates.

They arrived back just a day too late to catch the people who had been waiting for them, and who had finally given up on waiting that very morning. It seems they then completely jettisoned their common sense, probably because they were in the grip of scurvy. Whatever the cause, they muddled around for three weeks, wandering this way and that. In mid-May, they 'planted the things' and prepared to set out for Mount Hopeless, on a route that had worked well for Augustus Gregory not too long before. It took them two wasted days to do this, and then the following day they found they still had too much, and 'planted' some more. By then it was too late: their boots were worn out, they had nothing to use for repairs, no way of going anywhere.

The Burke and Wills party may have been the first Australian camel-eaters when they did so in March 1861. As Burke, Wills, Gray and King came down to Cooper's Creek, they stopped to kill and jerk Boocha the camel. At the end of April, they found another camel, Landa, caught in a waterhole and unable to get out, so Landa also became jerked camel meat.

By the middle of May 1861, the local Aborigines had introduced them to a staple of the local diet, nardoo (a water fern known to scientists as *Marsilea*, but known to Aboriginal people as a food source), the camel meat was running low, and Wills was devising plans to trap birds and 'rats', the small desert marsupial equivalents of rodents that were common in those days. In fact it was not until mid-June that they finished the camel Rajah, though King shot a crow to add to the larder. Wills was also prepared to try new foods, and here he wrote of what German botanist Ferdinand von Mueller later identified tentatively as *Muckia micrantha*.

> I observed on its banks two wild plants of the gourd or melon tribe, one much resembling a stunted cucumber: the other, both in leaf and appearance of fruit, was very similar to a small model of a water melon. The latter plant I also found at Camp 68. On tasting the pulp of the newly-found fruit, which was about the size of a large pea, I found it to be so acrid that it was with difficulty that I removed the taste from my mouth.

Wills once deprived some crows of a dead fish they were consuming, so as to eat it himself together with nardoo porridge.

At the end of May 1861, with less than a month to live, and his strength rapidly falling away, Wills struggled back to the DIG tree to deposit 'some journals and a notice of our present condition'. He noted that he was leaving them there 'for fear of accident', but there can be little doubt that his aim was to ensure that fame did not entirely elude him. A day or two before he died, he wrote a letter so it might be planted for later recovery.

For the most part, though, the explorers of Australia kept a stiff upper lip, while feeding enough evidence of their privations to their readers to show how they had suffered. After the travel, writing the journal was show business.

We have to assume that where an explorer got safely back to what passed for civilization, the published journals would have undergone some degree of editing to achieve the right effect, or that the journals were written from the start, as a ship's log was, often leaving a deal unsaid. The notebooks of the explorers were likely to be far more candid, and in a number of cases they reveal a degree of desperation about what posterity will make of the writer.

The journal of the Victorian Exploring Expedition (VEE) was never recovered, though the notebooks of John Wills were found. They were then filtered through the crusading intervention of Wills' father, determined to make sure that his son's name was never sullied in any way. Wills senior had to make do with the available scraps, but the comments of both non-planner Burke and his unplanned second-in-command paint a similar picture of awareness that their end was coming.

Wills senior did a neat hatchet job on Burke, reproducing a letter his son wrote to his mother. In this, Wills junior noted that none of the potential leaders had been chosen, because they lacked scientific qualifications. Then the father added, 'Oddly enough, Mr. Burke, who was afterwards chosen, with many requisites of a high order, was deficient in this, which, indeed, he never for a moment pretended to possess.'

All things considered, that is probably a fair comment, but when we look at the morale of the VEE, or the lack of it, we must understand that these were men exhausted, worn out, and almost certainly suffering from scurvy, so that even when they obtained food, or were given food by the remarkably caring Aborigines, it could do little good. Their morale was poor, but with good reason: they were dying, and seem to have recognized this.

On 23 June 1861, Wills is quoted as writing, 'All hands at home. I am so weak as to be incapable of crawling out of the mia-mia. King holds out well, but Mr. Burke finds himself weaker every day', while Burke, five days later, wrote, 'King has behaved nobly. He has stayed with me to the last, and placed the pistol in my hand, leaving me lying on the surface as I wished. R. O'H. Burke, Cooper's Creek, June 28th.'

The following day, Wills mentioned in his last entry that Burke was unwell, but did not say anything of his death. They must both have died around 29 June, though Wills seems to have been less aware that the end was near than Burke had been the previous day.

> My pulse is at forty-eight, and very weak, and my legs and arms are nearly skin and bone. I can only look out, like Mr. Micawber, 'for *something to turn* up;' starvation on nardoo is by no means very unpleasant, but for the weakness one feels, and the utter inability to move one's self; for as far as appetite is concerned, it gives the greatest satisfaction. Certainly fat and sugar would be more to one's taste; in fact those seem to me to be the great stand-by for one in this extraordinary continent: not that I mean to depreciate the farinaceous food; but the want of sugar and fat in all substances obtainable here is so great that they become almost valueless to us as articles of food, without the addition of something else.

THE EXPLORERS
WHO NEVER WERE

A couple of decades after William Dampier's account of Australia was published, Australia's coasts were supposedly visited by one Lemuel Gulliver, the hero of Jonathan Swift's *Gulliver's Travels*. Gulliver's Lilliput, the land of tiny people, was located by Swift as north-west of Van Diemen's Land (Tasmania), and in latitude 30°2'S, which places it not far from Woomera in South Australia, in an area traversed by Herschel Babbage.

In the tradition of Gulliver comes Louis de Rougemont, whose real name was Henri Louis Grin. His invented experiences began appearing in print in 1898, and his yarns included his life with an Aboriginal tribe who worshipped him as a god, his ride on a turtle, flying wombats and more. Before long, he was exposed as a fake.

Some 'explorers who never were' actually existed, like Mungo Park, who never quite arrived to solve the riddles of the outback, and Clarke the barber, with his story of the Kindur River, must have seen a few small bits of the tale he concocted. William Bland was a Sydney surgeon who proposed an 'atmotic ship', a hydrogen balloon powered by steam-driven propellers, in the 1850s. Mainly intended for the Sydney to London trade, the balloon would have moved swiftly over the deserts but, at 50 miles per hour (80 kilometres an hour), not so swiftly as to prevent a close examination of the land below. His balloon never flew.

There were other, even wilder schemes. Conrad Malte-Brun was a Danish-born French (by adoption) geographer who died in 1826, but before he died, he proposed that Australian explorers needed to take almost a circus with them.

> They should have oxen from Buenos Ayres, or from the
> English settlements, mules from Senegal, and dromedaries
> from Africa or Arabia ... Dogs also should be taken to raise

game, and to discover springs of water; and ... pigs, for the sake of finding out esculent roots in the soil. When no kangaroos and game are to be found the party would subsist on the flesh of their own flocks. They should be provided with a balloon for spying at a distance any serious obstacle to their progress in particular directions ... The journey might be allowed a year or eighteen months, which would be only at the rate of four or five miles per day ...

The idea of balloon-borne pigs seeking roots and maybe truffles in the arid plains of central Australia may have a certain piquancy, but the one thing practical explorers were agreed on was that you needed to use just one species of animal to carry the load, or face the risk of being hampered in turn by the shortcomings of each one. All the same, the Malte-Brun exploration model has a definite entertainment value, and when you look at some of the genuine heroes and fools who lurched and stumbled around and through Australia, who would dare call Malte-Brun's proposal far-fetched?

†

Dramatis personae

ARABANOO

Arabanoo (c. 1758–89): An Aboriginal man, captured near Sydney, and taught something of European ways, in an attempt to bridge the gap between two cultures. He was only able to travel briefly with one party before he died of a disease, most probably smallpox, in May 1789.

BABBAGE

Benjamin Herschel Babbage (1815–78): The son of computer pioneer Charles Babbage, he was a scientist rather than an explorer and showed a scientific approach to exploration, but achieved no important results in his 1856 and 1858 trips in South Australia. He was careful and methodical, taking everything that was required to observe, measure and record, even photographic equipment (in 1858!), as you might expect of somebody named after Sir John Herschel, a famous astronomer and photographer who invented the word 'photography'.

BANKS

Joseph Banks (1743–1820): Botanist who accompanied James **Cook** on his 1770 visit to the Australian coast and, as the powerful Sir Joseph Banks, influenced many later expeditions.

BARRALLIER

Francis Barrallier (1773–1853): French-born engineer who was one of the party under **Grant** which mapped the Hunter River (the site of Newcastle) in 1801. He tried to cross the Blue Mountains in 1802 on an embassy to a mythical 'King of the Mountains', a subterfuge of Governor **King** to justify sending a soldier exploring. Barrallier's mapping skills were rather limited.

BASS

George Bass (1771–1803): A surgeon, he sailed with Matthew Flinders in the *Tom Thumb* in 1795, tried to cross the Blue Mountains in 1795–96, and with **Flinders** discovered what is now Bass Strait, in 1798. He later disappeared mysteriously in South America.

BAUDIN

Thomas Nicolas Baudin (1754–1803): He commanded the French ships *Géographe* and *Naturaliste* in 1801–03, on Australian coasts.

BAUER

Ferdinand Lukas Bauer (1760–1826): An Austrian-born botanical artist who travelled with Matthew **Flinders** in HMS *Investigator*, 1801–03. He returned to Europe in 1805.

BAXTER

John (or James) Baxter (unknown–1841): He was **Eyre**'s overseer for many years. He was shot and killed by two Aboriginal servants on the Great Australian Bight in 1841. Little is known of him.

BIRTLES

Francis Birtles (1881–1941): The first person to cross the Nullarbor on a bicycle, and he later did so again in a car.

BLAXLAND

Gregory Blaxland (1778–1853): He came to Australia as a settler in 1805 and later joined **Wentworth** and **Lawson** in the celebrated crossing of the Blue Mountains in 1813.

BONNEY

Charles Bonney (1813–97): One of the earliest overlanders, he found a stock route to Melbourne in early 1837, and was with the first cattle taken from New South Wales to Adelaide in 1838. He later settled in Adelaide and was later a member of parliament.

BROWN

Robert Brown (1773–1858): A botanist who was originally a surgeon's mate. He travelled with Matthew **Flinders** in HMS *Investigator* and independently, 1801–05, collecting specimens of Australian plants for Sir Joseph **Banks**. Among biologists, his lasting fame comes from his discovery of the nucleus, while chemists and physicists recall his discovery of Brownian motion.

An Aboriginal man from the Newcastle area called Brown accompanied **Leichhardt**. No dates are known for him.

BUCHANAN

Nat Buchanan (1826–1901): Born in Dublin, Buchanan came to Australia in 1837. He was an excellent bushman who found a path from the Overland Telegraph line to western Queensland. He was in the field from 1859 to 1896, when he travelled the Tanami Desert from Tennant Creek to Halls Creek. His fame came from his skill at finding new routes and droving cattle across country.

BUNDELL

Bundell (c. 1790–unknown, possibly post-1843): An Aborigine who accompanied Phillip Parker **King**, in place of Bungaree, in 1821.

BUNGAREE, BONGAREE, BOONGAREE

Bungaree (c. 1772–1830): An Aboriginal man from Broken Bay, he sailed with **Flinders**, 1799 and 1801–3, and with Phillip Parker **King** in the north-west of Australia in 1817.

BURKE

Robert O'Hara Burke (1821–61): Formerly an officer in the Austrian army, though born in Ireland, Burke came to Australia and became a policeman and then the inept leader of the Burke and **Wills** expedition, 1860–61.

CALEY

George Caley (1770–1829): A botanical collector who tried to cross the Blue Mountains in 1804. He was a good worker, but had an unfortunate personality, which limited his effectiveness.

CARNEGIE

David Wynford Carnegie (1871–1900): Gold prospector and desert traveller in Western Australia in the 1890s. The fourth son of an earl, he considered that if there was gold at Coolgardie and at Halls Creek, there ought to be some in between, so he crossed Australia the hard way, through the Gibson Desert and the Great Sandy Desert. He and his party returned to the east of their first route, covering a total distance of some 4800 kilometres in thirteen months.

CARRON

William Carron (1821–76): A botanist, survivor of the ill-fated **Kennedy** expedition of 1847–48. He later worked in the government service in customs, at Sydney's Botanic Gardens, and then in forestry.

CHARLEY

Charley (dates unknown): An Aborigine from the Bathurst region, he accompanied **Leichhardt** on his first expedition.

CLARKE

George Clarke (dates unknown): A runaway convict, known as 'the barber', who told a wild tale of a river called the Kindur, prompting **Mitchell**'s 1831–32 expedition.

There was also a geologist, W.B. Clarke, who found the first gold specimens in New South Wales in 1844, but the find was hushed up, for fear that chaos would result.

COOK

James Cook (1728–79): English mariner and navigator who successfully mapped the eastern coast of Australia in 1770, from Point Hicks to Cape York, and formally claimed that side of the continent for Britain. He visited Tahiti and New Zealand first and, with his crew, survived severe damage to his ship on the Great Barrier Reef.

CREAGHE

Emily Caroline Creaghe (1861–1944): The only woman member of Ernest **Favenc**'s exploration of northern Australia in 1883. She was more a traveller than an explorer, but her efforts were equal to those of many explorers.

CUNNINGHAM

Allan Cunningham (1791–1839): Botanist and explorer who was sent to Australia on a recommendation from **Banks**. He worked mainly in New South Wales (1817, 1823, 1827) and southern Queensland (1828), and on the coast with P.P. **King** (1817–22).

His brother Richard (1792–1833) was also a botanist: he died on Sir Thomas **Mitchell**'s second expedition. Allan had returned to England in 1831, but returned later to replace his brother as colonial botanist at Sydney's Botanic Gardens, where his remains were placed in 1901.

DAMPIER
William Dampier (1652–1715): The first Englishman to land in New Holland in 1688, and again in 1699. A number of features near Broome still bear names that he gave them. Possibly born in 1651.

DARKE
John Charles Darke (1806–44): A surveyor and minor explorer who was speared by Aborigines on the Eyre Peninsula while out looking for good land that was said to be there.

DAWES
William Dawes (1762–1836): Lieutenant in the Marines with the First Fleet. Crossed the Nepean in 1789 and explored south and west of Rosehill in 1790, with **Tench**. Dawes carried out astronomical observations at the point that bears his name in Sydney, and built an artillery battery there. He was an early authority on the local Aboriginal languages and might have remained in Australia, but he quarrelled with Governor Phillip.

D'ENTRECASTEAUX
Joseph-Antoine Raymond Bruny d'Entrecasteaux (1739–93): Left Brest in 1791 to seek **La Pérouse**, with the ships *Recherche* and *L'Esperance*, and was in Australian waters, 1792–93.

EURANABIE
Euranabie (dates unknown): Euranabie (or Yeranabie) and his wife Worogan sailed in the *Lady Nelson* under **Grant** to Jervis Bay

and Bass Strait in March 1801. He was expected to act as an interpreter.

EVANS

George William Evans (1780–1852): Sent to map the land across the Blue Mountains in 1813, second-in-command in **Oxley**'s 1817 and 1818 expeditions. He worked as a surveyor after that, but in the 1830s he was a Sydney bookseller and stationer before moving to Hobart, where he died.

EYRE

Edward John Eyre (1815–1901): Overlanded stock from New South Wales to both Melbourne and Adelaide, explored in South Australia, walked along the Great Australian Bight in 1840–41, was later lieutenant-governor in New Zealand and governor in Jamaica.

FAVENC

Ernest Favenc (1845–1908): Explorer, writer and journalist, also a minor explorer in the 1870s and 1880s.

FLINDERS

Matthew Flinders (1774–1814): Royal Navy officer who explored part of the New South Wales coast with George **Bass** in the *Tom Thumb*, later explored Bass Strait with Bass, and in HMS *Investigator* charted much of the Australian coast, 1801–03.

FORREST

John Forrest (1847–1918): Searched for **Leichhardt** in 1869, crossed from Perth to Adelaide in 1870 and surveyed the route of the Overland Telegraph in 1874.

His brother Alexander (1849–1901) was second-in-command to John in the north-west of Australia and explored the Hampton Plains in 1871 and 1876. John was later knighted, then became the first Baron Forrest of Bunbury.

FREYCINET

Louis-Claude Saulces de Freycinet (1779–1842): Sailed with **Baudin** (1801–03), who gave him command of the *Casuarina,* and commanded the *Uranie* from 1817, when he stole de **Vlamingh**'s plate from Dirk Hartog Island and took it back to Paris. The plate was only returned to Australia after World War II.

Freycinet's wife Rose (1794–1832) stowed away on his ship and sailed with him until 1820.

GIBSON

Alfred Gibson (unknown–1873): Died on **Giles**' second expedition, in what is now the Gibson Desert.

GILES

Ernest Giles (1835–97): Made a number of attempts between 1872 and 1876 to force a way through central Australia and down to Perth, eventually succeeding in travelling both directions. It was a major achievement, but he found nothing of value and failed to gain any real public recognition, unlike **Warburton**.

GILL

S.T. (Samuel Thomas) Gill (1818–80): Artist who reached South Australia in 1839. He travelled as an unpaid draughtsman on John **Horrocks'** fatal expedition in 1846. His notes on the expedition were published in *The South Australian Gazette and Colonial Register* on 10 October 1846, and he later exhibited a number of paintings; at least 33 were in existence in February 1847. He was later on the Victorian goldfields and in Sydney before settling in Melbourne.

GIRARGIN

Louis Girargin (c. 1743–94): In reality, Louise Girargin, a 38-year-old steward on **d'Entrecasteaux's** ship, visiting Australian waters 1792–93.

GRANT

Lieutenant James Grant, RN (1772–1833): Master of the first vessel to pass through Bass Strait in 1801, he then took Francis **Barrallier** and others to map parts of the southern coast and also the Hunter River, in 1801. A seaman rather than a mapmaker.

GREGORY

Augustus Charles Gregory (1819–1905): Leader of the North Australian Exploring Expedition 1854–58, which went looking for **Leichhardt** or his remains, and surveyor-general of Queensland from 1859.

His brothers Francis Thomas (Frank) Gregory (1821–88) and Henry Churchman Gregory (1823–69) travelled with Augustus on a short trip in 1846, then Frank followed the Gascoyne River to Shark Bay in 1858. Frank Gregory also traced the Murchison down to Geraldton, and explored areas in north-western Australia. Henry was second-in-command of the North Australian Expedition.

GREY
Lieutenant George Grey (1812–98): A soldier and untrained explorer who took dangerous risks, which led to injury and death within his party on several expeditions in 1837 and 1838 in parts of what is now Western Australia. He was at one stage governor of South Australia.

HARRIS
John Harris (1754–1838): A naval surgeon, he went on the Hunter River expedition of 1801, and in 1818 he volunteered to accompany John **Oxley** on his expedition from Bathurst to Port Macquarie and Newcastle.

HAWDON
Joseph Hawdon (1813–71): One of the earliest overlanders, taking stock from the established pastoral runs in New South Wales to Victoria and South Australia in the 1830s.

HODDLE
Robert Hoddle (1794–1881): A surveyor, he laid out roads into the Blue Mountains and travelled with Oxley in Queensland in the

1820s, later working widely as a surveyor on the New South Wales south coast and in Victoria, where he laid out part of Melbourne.

HORROCKS

John Ainsworth Horrocks (1818–46): An English explorer who was shot by his camel while searching for farming land.

HOVELL

William Hovell (1786–1875): A sea captain who travelled with Hamilton **Hume** from near Lake George to Port Phillip in 1824–25. Hovell had little experience in the bush, but was skilled as a navigator, while Hume lacked the ability to determine a position.

HUME

Hamilton Hume (1797–1873): Australian-born, Hume is best known for travelling with **Hovell** to Port Phillip. Hume also accompanied **Sturt** on his first expedition into western New South Wales.

JACKEY JACKEY

Jackey Jackey (unknown–1854): Also called Jackey, an Aboriginal guide and assistant, one of the three survivors of the 1847 **Kennedy** expedition, a man who was repeatedly praised for his devotion to Kennedy. He was probably born no earlier than 1830, and died after he fell into a campfire while drunk.

JARDINE

Francis Lascelles Jardine (1841–1919): With his brother, Alexander, he overlanded cattle to Somerset (Cape York) in 1864–65.

KENNEDY

Edmund Besley Court Kennedy (1813–48): Best known as the leader of an ill-conceived expedition to travel overland to Cape York in 1847–48. He had previously done some useful work.

KING

There are three Kings in this narrative: the third colonial governor, Philip Gidley King; his son, Phillip Parker King (1791–1856, born at Norfolk Island); and an unrelated undersecretary of state, John King. The only explorer among them was P.P. King, an officer in the Royal Navy, who mapped Australia's coasts extensively between 1817 and 1822. He later helped map Tierra del Fuego when Darwin was there on the *Beagle*, and became an admiral.

There was also John King, an Irish soldier who was the only member of the Burke and Wills party to see salt water on the north coast of Australia and survive to tell the tale.

LA PÉROUSE

Jean-François de Galaup, Comte de La Pérouse (1741–88): The commander of a French expedition sent to explore the Pacific in 1785. He called at Botany Bay, within days of the arrival of the First Fleet, but his ships were wrecked near Vanikoro, and all on board died, either in the wreck or after leaving to seek help, or on the island itself. The fate of La Pérouse remains a mystery.

LANDELLS

George James Landells (1825–1871): The camelmaster and original second-in-command of the Burke and Wills expedition. Offended by Burke's decision to get rid of the rum that Landells thought would save the camels from scurvy, he resigned at Menindie.

LANDSBOROUGH

William Landsborough (1825–86): Led the Queensland search party for **Burke** and **Wills** in 1861–62. Starting from the mouth of the Albert River, in the Gulf of Carpentaria, they finally reached Melbourne after an epic journey.

LAWSON

William Lawson (1774–1850): Lawson travelled over the Blue Mountains with **Blaxland** and **Wentworth** in 1813, and took the first stock over the mountains in 1815.

LEICHHARDT

Ludwig Leichhardt (1813–48?): German naturalist who arrived in Sydney in 1842. He made one successful expedition of some fifteen months (1844–45) and two failed ones, perishing on the second of his failed attempts to cross Australia from east to west.

MACGILLIVRAY

John Macgillivray (1821–67): A naturalist on HMS *Rattlesnake* in Australian and New Guinea waters, 1846–50. He later settled in Australia and died at Grafton.

MCINTYRE

Duncan McIntyre (1831–66): He travelled from the Paroo to the Gulf of Carpentaria in 1864, and was part of the ill-fated 'Ladies' Leichhardt Search Expedition' in 1865.

MITCHELL

Sir Thomas Livingstone Mitchell (1792–1855): Major Mitchell, as he originally was, had served in the Peninsular War in Spain and Portugal. He approached exploration as a military activity. In 1831–32, he mapped some of the rivers found previously by **Oxley**. In 1836, he worked down into Victoria, discovering the area he dubbed 'Australia Felix', and in 1845–46 led an expedition to the Barcoo.

M'MILLAN

Angus M'Millan (1810–65): Also seen as McMillan. He explored the Australian Alps and Gippsland in 1840.

MUELLER

Ferdinand von Mueller (or Müller) (1825–96): A German botanist who trained first as a pharmacist, he explored the Australian Alps in 1846–47, travelled with **Gregory**'s North Australia Expedition of 1855–56, and advised many other explorers on their plant and animal collections. He sponsored the Victorian Exploring Expedition of **Burke** and **Wills** and 'The Ladies' Leichhardt Search Expedition' of **McIntyre**.

MURRAY

Lieutenant John Murray (c. 1775–unknown): He succeeded James **Grant** in command of the *Lady Nelson*, and discovered Port Phillip while exploring Bass Strait in 1802.

There was also a Dr James Murray who was the second-in-command of **McIntyre**'s expedition and caused its collapse.

OXLEY

John Molesworth Oxley (1785?–1828): Originally a naval officer, Oxley served in Australian waters for several years. After he took up the post of surveyor-general of New South Wales in 1812, his expeditions included travels along the Lachlan and Macquarie rivers in 1817, and a further attempt (1817–18) that saw him swing east around the Warrumbungles, over the Great Dividing Range to Port Macquarie, and down the coast to Newcastle. He examined Jervis Bay and Port Macquarie by sea, and in 1823 the Moreton Bay area.

PATERSON

Lieutenant-Colonel William Paterson (1755–1810): Paterson made several expeditions, notably the exploration of the lower waters of the Hunter River in 1801 with **Grant** and **Barrallier**. He collected plants for **Banks** from 1781, and sent him plant, rock and animal specimens from Norfolk Island. Governor **King** later made him lieutenant-governor. He sailed for England in 1810, but died at sea.

PHILLIP

Arthur Phillip (1738–1814): The first governor of the infant colony at Sydney, Phillip undertook or sent several short expeditions to explore the immediate vicinity of the colony between 1788 and 1790. He returned to England in 1792 and became a rear admiral of the Blue in 1799, later admiral of the Blue, shortly before his death.

ROE

John Septimus Roe (1797–1878): A midshipman in the *Mermaid* with **King**, he sailed for the Swan River as surveyor-general in 1829, and served the colony in that role until 1860. He was sent out at one stage to save the party led by **Grey**.

STOKES

John Lort Stokes (1812–85): Originally a lieutenant on HMS *Beagle* when Charles Darwin sailed in her, he became the ship's commander in a later voyage. He surveyed the Australian coast from 1837 to 1845.

STRZELECKI

Paul Edmund de Strzelecki (1797–1873): He visited Gippsland after **M'Millan** and climbed the Alps, and named one of the highest peaks Kosciuszko, from its fancied resemblance to the Polish patriot's tomb at Cracow.

STUART

John McDouall Stuart (1815–66): Gained experience as the draughtsman of **Sturt**'s 1844 expedition, worked as a surveyor in South Australia and succeeded on his sixth and last expedition of 1861–62 in crossing the continent from south to north and returning alive, though in poor health.

STURT

Charles Sturt (1795–1869): He went to western New South Wales with **Hume** during a drought in 1828–29, and reached the Darling River. In 1829–30, he sailed down the Murray and found where the Darling River joined the Murray. His third expedition, in 1844–46, was an attempt to find a way into central Australia, west of the Darling.

TASMAN

Abel Janszoon Tasman (1603–59): Sailed round much of the Australian coast, often at a distance, sighted what he called Van Diemen's Land, now Tasmania, and New Zealand.

TENCH

Watkin Tench (c. 1758–1833): Captain-lieutenant of Marines, he came to Sydney in the First Fleet, and explored the Hawkesbury and Nepean rivers in 1789 and 1790. He returned to Britain in 1791 and later published two books on the colony. He later reached the rank of lieutenant-general.

TOMMY

Giles had an Aboriginal companion of this name. See also Tommy **Winditj**.

WARBURTON

Peter Warburton (1813–89): Replaced Herschel **Babbage** in 1857, and undertook an expedition from the Overland Telegraph line at Alice Springs to the Oakover River in Western Australia in

1872–73. He found no exploitable land, and those who came after him found his maps useless, but the English public made a hero of him.

WENTWORTH
William Charles Wentworth (1790–1872): One of the three named Europeans who crossed the Blue Mountains in 1813, along with some servants.

WILLS
William John Wills (1834–61): Originally the surveyor, astronomer and third-in-command, he became the second-in-command of what is now known as the **Burke** and Wills expedition. When Burke decided to push ahead to Cooper's Creek with a smaller party, leaving others to catch up, Wills was with him. When Burke decided to push ahead with an even smaller group, Wills accompanied him again, and later died within a few days of Burke.

WILSON
John Wilson (unknown–1800): Sometimes identified as James, he was a convict who took to the bush when his term expired. He spent a lot of time with the Aborigines near Sydney in the early days, and guided a 1798 expedition that probably reached the Wingecarribee River and got as far as modern Goulburn. He travelled further than any other European up to the time of his death.

Edward Wilson was a blacksmith with Mitchell, and one J.S. Wilson was a somewhat difficult geologist on one of Augustus Gregory's trips.

WINDITJ

Tommy Winditj (1840–76): Also referred to as Windich. An Aborigine from near Mount Stirling in Western Australia, he travelled on several of the Forrest expeditions between 1869 and 1876. He died of pneumonia while guiding a party building a telegraph line from Adelaide to Perth.

WOROGAN

Worogan (dates unknown): The Aboriginal wife of **Euranabie**, she sailed in the *Lady Nelson* to Jervis Bay and Bass Strait.

WYLIE

Wylie (dates unknown, died later than 1848): An Aborigine from the Albany area of Western Australia, who assisted and supported **Eyre** in his walk around the Great Australian Bight in 1840–41.

YERANABIE

See **Euranabie**.

✠

OFF-STAGE PLAYERS

A few explorers do not figure in this story, but they still matter.

HAMELIN

Jacques Felix Emmanuel Hamelin (1768–1839): A member of the 1801–03 expedition commanded by Nicolas **Baudin**. He had de **Vlamingh**'s plate attached to a new post and left on Dirk Hartog Island, which annoyed **Freycinet**, who later stole it.

HARTOG

Dirk Hartog (dates unknown): The captain of the *Eendracht*, he came ashore on Dirk Hartog Island in October 1616. He left a pewter plate with an inscription as evidence of his visit.

PÉRON

François Péron (1775–1810): Naturalist on **Baudin**'s 1801–03 expedition.

VLAMINGH

Willem de Vlamingh (1640–unknown): He found **Hartog**'s plate in 1697, damaged but legible. He had the text copied onto a new plate, added his own inscription and sailed off, taking the original back to the Netherlands—appropriately, because de Vlamingh and Hartog were of the same nation and a replacement plate was left behind.

Bibliography

Anonymous, 'Return of His Excellency—Report of the Expedition by the Hon. Capt Sturt', *South Australian Register*, 4 January 1840. State Library of South Australia, http://www.slsa.sa.gov.au/murray/content/europeanDiscovery/ saRegister4jan1840_pg3.htm, last accessed 30 December 2004.

Appleyard, Ron, Barbara Fargher & Ron Radford, *S.T. Gill: the South Australian Years, 1839–1852*. Adelaide: Art Gallery of South Australia, 1986.

Bach, John (ed.), *The Bligh Notebook*. Sydney: Allen & Unwin with the National Library of Australia, 1987.

Barton, G.B., *History of New South Wales from the Records, volume I*. Sydney: Charles Potter, Government Printer, 1889.

Blaxland, Gregory, *The Journal of Gregory Blaxland*, 1813 (published 1913). Project Gutenberg: http://gutenberg.net.au/ebooks02/0200411.txt, last accessed 31 May 2007.

Brown, Lloyd A., *The Story of Maps*. New York: Dover Publications, 1977.

Carnegie, David, *Spinifex and Sand*, http://freeread.com.au/ebooks/e00042.html, last accessed 31 May 2007.

Carpenter, Kenneth J., *The History of Scurvy and Vitamin C*. Cambridge: Cambridge University Press, 1986.

Carron, William, *Narrative of an Expedition Undertaken under the Direction of E.B. Kennedy* (1849) http://gutenberg.net.au/ebooks02/0201121.txt, last accessed 31 May 2007.

—, *Narrative of an Expedition, Undertaken under the Direction of the Late Mr. Assistant Surveyor E.B. Kennedy, for the Exploration of the Country Lying between Rockingham Bay and Cape York*, Sydney: Kemp and Fairfax, 1849.

Coats, R.P. & A.H. Blissett, *Regional and Economic Geology of the Mount Painter Province*, Bulletin 43. Adelaide: Department of Mines, Geological Survey of South Australia, 1971.

Collins, David, *An Account of the English Colony in New South Wales* (2 vols). Sydney: A.H. and A.W. Reed, 1975.

Cook, James, *Captain Cook's Journal during the First Voyage round the World Made in H.M. Bark Endeavour*. http://freeread.com.au/ebooks/e00043.html, last accessed 31 May 2007.

—, *The Voyages of Captain Cook*. Ware: Wordsworth Classics, 1999.

Cordingly, David, *Captain James Cook, Navigator*. London: National Maritime Museum, 1988.

Dampier, William, *A New Voyage round the World*. Project Gutenberg: http://gutenberg.net.au/ebooks05/0500461.txt, last accessed 31 May 2007.

—, *A Voyage to New Holland, etc in the Year 1699.*
http://freeread.com.au/ebooks/e00046.html, last accessed
31 May 2007.

Dick, Oliver Lawson (ed.), *Aubrey's Brief Lives.* Harmondsworth: Penguin
Books, 1976.

Eyre, Edward John, *Journals of Expeditions of Discovery into Central
Australia, etc.*, Volumes 1 and 2.
http://freeread.com.au/ebooks/e00048.html, last accessed
31 May 2007.

Fisher, Dennis, *Latitude Hooks and Azimuth Rings.* Camden, Maine:
International Marine, 1995.

Flinders, Matthew, *A Voyage to Terra Australis*, Volumes 1 and 2.
http://freeread.com.au/ebooks/e00049.html and
http://freeread.com.au/ebooks/e00050.html, last accessed
31 May 2007.

Forrest, John & Alexander, *Explorations in Australia.*
http://freeread.com.au/ebooks/e00051.html, last accessed
31 May 2007.

Giles, Ernest, *Australia Twice Traversed.*
http://freeread.com.au/ebooks/e00052.html, last accessed
31 May 2007.

—, *Australia Twice Traversed, the Romance of Exploration.*
London: Sampson Low, Marston, Searle & Rivington,
1889.

Gregory, Augustus Charles & Francis Thomas, *Journals of Australian
Exploration*, Brisbane, 1884.

Gregory, Frank & Augustus, *Journals of Australian Exploration.*
http://freeread.com.au/ebooks/e00053.html, last accessed
31 May 2007.

Grey, George, *Journals of Two Expeditions of Discovery in North-West and Western Australia*. http://freeread.com.au/ebooks/e00054.html and http://freeread.com.au/ebooks/e00055.html, last accessed 31 May 2007.

—, *Journals of Two Expeditions of Discovery in North-West and Western Australia during the Years 1837, 38 and 39*. London: T. & W. Boone, 1841.

Hordern, Marsden, *King of the Australian Coast: the work of Phillip Parker King in the Mermaid and Bathurst 1817–1822*. Carlton: Melbourne University Press, 1997.

—, *Mariners are Warned! John Lort Stokes and HMS Beagle in Australia 1837–1843*. Carlton: Melbourne University Press, 1989.

Hovell, William & Hamilton Hume, *Journey of Discovery to Port Phillip*. Project Gutenberg: http://gutenberg.net.au/ebooks04/0400371.txt, last accessed 31 May 2007.

Huxley, Julian (ed.), *T.H. Huxley's Diary of the Voyage of H. M. S. Rattlesnake*. London: Chatto and Windus, 1935.

Jardine, Alexander & Frank, *Narrative of the Overland Expedition of the Messrs Jardine, from Rockhampton to Cape York, Northern Queensland*. http://freeread.com.au/ebooks/e00026.html, last accessed 31 May 2007.

Kabaila, Peter, *High Country Footprints: Aboriginal pathways and movement in the high country of southeastern Australia*. Canberra: Pirion Publishing, 2005.

King, Phillip Parker, *Narrative of a Survey of the Intertropical and Western Coasts of Australia*, Volumes 1 and 2. http://freeread.com.au/ebooks/e00027.html and http://freeread.com.au/ebooks/e00028.html, last accessed 31 May 2007.

Landsborough, William, *Journal of Landsborough's Expedition from Carpentaria, in Search of Burke and Wills*, 1862. http://freeread.com.au/ebooks/e00029.html, last accessed 31 May 2007.

Leichhardt, Ludwig, *Journal of an Overland Expedition in Australia 1844–1845* http://freeread.com.au/ebooks/e00030.html, last accessed 31 May 2007.

—, *Journal of an Overland Expedition in Australia from Moreton Bay to Port Essington during the Years 1844–1845*, 1 volume and maps. London, 1847.

Mabey, David & Robin Bailey, 'Perspective: Eradication of trachoma worldwide', *British Journal of Ophthalmology*, 1999; 83:1261–1263. http://bjo.bmjjournals.com/cgi/content/full/83/11/1261#B6, last accessed 6 June 2007.

Macgillivray, John, *Narrative of the Voyage of H.M.S. Rattlesnake, 1846–50*, Volumes 1 and 2. http://freeread.com.au/ebooks/e00031.html and http://freeread.com.au/ebooks/e00032.html, last accessed 31 May 2007.

Macinnis, Peter, *Climbing Mt Exmouth*. http://www.abc.net.au/rn/ockhamsrazor/stories/2006/1774279.htm, last accessed 31 May 2007.

McKinlay, John, *McKinlay's Journal of Exploration in the Interior of Australia (Burke Relief Expedition)*. http://freeread.com.au/ebooks/e00033.txt, last accessed 31 May 2007.

Mitchell, Thomas, *Journal of an Expedition into the Interior of Tropical Australia*. http://freeread.com.au/ebooks/e00034.html, last accessed 31 May 2007.

—, *Three Expeditions into the Interior of Eastern Australia*, Volumes 1 and 2. http://freeread.com.au/ebooks/e00035.html and http://freeread.com.au/ebooks/e00036.html, last accessed 31 May 2007.

Oxley, John, *Journals of Two Expeditions into the Interior of New South Wales*. http://freeread.com.au/ebooks/e00037.txt, last accessed 31 May 2007.

Shaw, W. Hudson & Olaf Ruhen, *Lawrence Hargrave*. Sydney: Cassell Australia, 1977.

Smyth, Arthur Bowes, *The Journal of Arthur Bowes Smyth* (edited by Paul Fidlon and R.J. Ryan). Sydney: Australian Documents Library, 1979.

Stanbury, Peter (ed.), *100 Years of Australian Scientific Explorations*. Sydney: Macleay Museum, c. 1975.

Stokes, Edward, *The Desert Coast: Edward Eyre's expedition 1840–41*. Knoxfield, Victoria: Five Mile Press, 1993.

Stokes, John Lort, *Discoveries in Australia, with an Account of the Coasts and Rivers Explored and Surveyed during the Voyage of H.M.S. Beagle, in the Years 1837–38–39–40–41–42–43. (Also a Narrative of Captain Owen Stanley's Visits to the Islands in the Arafura Sea.)*, Volumes 1 and 2. http://freeread.com.au/ebooks/e00038.html and http://freeread.com.au/ebooks/e00039.html, last accessed 31 May 2007.

Stuart, John McDouall, *Explorations in Australia*. http://freeread.com.au/ebooks/e00040.html, last accessed 31 May 2007.

—, *Explorations in Australia: The journals of John McDouall Stuart, during the years 1858–62*, 2nd edn. William Hardman (ed.), London, 1865.

Sturt, Charles, *Narrative of an Expedition into Central Australia*. http://freeread.com.au/ebooks/e00058.html, last accessed 31 May 2007.

—, *Narrative of an Expedition into Central Australia*, 2 volumes. London: T. & W. Boone, 1849.

—, *Two Expeditions into the Interior of Southern Australia*. http://freeread.com.au/ebooks/e00059.html, last accessed 31 May 2007.

Tasman, Abel, *The Journal of Abel Jansz Tasman, 1642, with Documents Relating to his Exploration of Australia in 1644*. http://gutenberg.net.au/ebooks04/0400771.txt, last accessed 31 May 2007.

Threadgill, Bessie, *South Australian Land Exploration, 1856 to 1880*. Adelaide: Board of Governors of the Public Library, Museum and Art Gallery of South Australia, 1922.

Villiers, Alan, *Captain Cook, The Seamen's Seaman*. Harmondsworth: Penguin Books, 1969.

Walker, Frederick, *Journal of Expedition in Search of Burke and Wills*. http://gutenberg.net.au/ebooks06/0600191.txt, last accessed 31 May 2007.

Waterton, Charles, *Wanderings in South America*. Project Gutenberg file 7wnsa10.txt, last accessed 30 August 2004.

Wills, William John, *Successful Exploration through the Interior of Australia*. http://freeread.com.au/ebooks/e00060.html, last accessed 31 May 2007.

✠

Acknowledgements

Dave Himsley taught me as a boy to walk quietly in the bush and appreciate the achievements of Aboriginal people. Andy Berriman, Tony Tucker and a former marine called Derek introduced me to wombat tracks in the Budawang ranges, and Col Watson taught me more about them. My family, Christine, Angus, Cate and Duncan, all indulged me as we poked around wombat tracks over the years.

Phil Gee introduced me to camels in central Australia; Julia Bell in Western Australia gave me some more first-hand information on camels and their habits; and in the Kimberley, Mark Schmidt of KWA aided me in getting some tropical ground truth and a better understanding of the geology. Kieran Kelly shared his researches into the Gregory compass with me. Many writers have shared their ideas by way of their books.

I must thank the State Library of New South Wales, particularly the Mitchell Library. The University of Sydney's Fisher Library was a joy, and I was helped greatly by Adelaide's Barr Smith Library, the South Australian Museum (especially Mark Pharaoh) and the Art Gallery of South Australia. In Fremantle, the Western Australian Maritime Museum and the Shipwreck Galleries provided some useful insights.

So many people have helped in so many ways—even the occupants of a small tavern at the intersection of Rue Lesueur and Rue Laperouse. They made Chris and I welcome in rainy, windswept, chilly Le Havre on a spring day where winter struck back, as the shop awnings dripped stickily after their annual scrubbing to redistribute the guano deposits contributed by the hardy seagulls.

We waited there for a museum to open so we could see Lesueur's Australian collections. It seemed like a set from *Irma La Douce*, so it came as no surprise to learn later what the main trade was in that part of the port of Le Havre. We must have seemed equally exotic to them, but we chatted in franglais, shared, and were advised. I probably learned more at the Musée de la Marine in Paris, but Le Havre, the port so many French explorers departed from, has fonder memories for me.

Reading about Australian exploration has become a great deal easier in recent years, thanks to Project Gutenberg and a few dedicated hands who have taken most of the rare and hard-to-find journals and put them into electronic form. Sue Asscher and Colin Choat are the most frequent names, but I know there are others who have given selflessly.

Then there are my friends who read a late draft and advised me kindly. My son Angus, David Allen in Queensland, Luke Owens in California, Dee Churchill in Oregon, and Lesley Knieriem in Arkansas have all worked their way through it, my tame Americans alerting me to places where I may have assumed too much knowledge in the reader. The remnant errors are mine alone.

I owe thanks also to the team at Murdoch Books who encouraged me to revisit an old interest. Diana Hill encouraged me. Anouska Jones searched my words, fearlessly and fiercely, hunting down inapposite remarks, clumsy wording and other clottish behaviour. In fairness to her, I did occasionally insist on archaic usages, gnomic comments and waspish remarks, but she truly did try to save me from myself. Then there are the design people who worked hard to make it all look good: Reuben Crossman did the cover, while Peter Long and Vivien Valk did the internal layout. There is more to making a book than the mere herding of words, and the whole team did me proud!

But I owe most to those who went out, came back, and told their stories, or kept their records, so they could be placed in a library somewhere. Without them, there would be no story to tell.